THE MYSTIC DREAM BOOK

D0827612

2500
Dreams Explained

LONDON
W. FOULSHAM & CO., LTD.
NEW YORK - TORONTO - CAPE TOWN - SYDNEY

W. FOULSHAM & CO. LTD.
Yeovil Road, Slough, Berks., England

ISBN 0-572-00207-6

Printed and bound in Great Britain by
Cox & Wyman Ltd., Reading, Berks.

THE MYSTIC DREAM BOOK

THERE are very few people who do not dream, though occasionally we come across people who can truthfully tell us that they have never known such an occurrence. In such cases we might be more correct if we assumed that, in actual fact, they do dream, but that they retain no conscious recollection of the event.

Before we begin to deal with the fascinating study of Dreams and their Interpretation, it is important to realise that these curious mental experiences belong to two very distinct classes—there are dreams which are merely the result of physical discomfort, either past or present, as well as others that might be better described as visions.

Any mental disturbance that is due to a purely physical cause cannot possibly carry a meaning, and must be ignored by those who wish to learn how to deal with real meanings. First among the physical dreams we can place those horrible experiences known as nightmares, which are almost always due to digestive trouble. This causes an irregular supply of blood to the brain, and also, no doubt, an impure supply. Either or both of these troubles will prove sufficient to cause nightmare, which can always be distinguished by the extravagance and impossibility of the happenings through which the Dreamer appears to pass.

There is, however, a great difference between *impossible* happenings and *improbable* events. The improbable dreams deserve investigation, for they are often of the nature of Visions, whereas the impossible can be ignored as due to some physical cause.

Sometimes, however, a perfectly possible event will figure as a Dream, yet it may be due to a simple physical cause. A man who was a strong believer in Dreams had a vivid experience one night, when he believed that he was out in the desert, pursued by a lion, who was so close to him all the time that the animal was constantly biting him in the thigh, though never able to overtake him.

When this man awoke he was in a state of profuse perspiration, and was deeply impressed by what he took to be a Vision of warning. Upon getting up, however, he found that, by some mistake, his false teeth had slipped between the sheets, so that in reality he had been biting himself all the time, thus inducing this particular dream.

In another case of persistent dreaming—this time a lady—we were told by the husband that the same ghastly dream came frequently to his wife, and that he always knew when this was the case because of her terrified screams.

Many people believe that a persistent dream—one in which the same incident is repeated, though the general details may vary to a great extent—must be a warning of deep importance. This is doubtful if the dream recurs more than a few times. In the case mentioned we found that the lady, as a schoolgirl, had been concerned in a most unpleasant incident, which resulted in two girls being expelled, though she herself escaped this fate. She had been so terrified at the thought of what her parents would have done if she herself had been publicly disgraced, that this dream had haunted her sleep ever since.

This proves that a *persistent* dream will almost always have a physical cause, due to some dramatic incident in the past ; whereas a dream that is merely repeated two or three times is a very different affair, and should be treated seriously.

The majority of dreams come to us during sleep, and

naturally this generally means at night. But many people who are highly sensitive receive these mental impressions quite easily when in the wakeful period of the day—even in the midst of some normal occupation. Such dreams are obviously Visions, or mental impressions received from some intimate friend or relation.

An actual experience will illustrate this type of dream. A musician had spent the week-end with some old friends in the country, but on arriving home on the Monday evening he had such a daydream, that included a doctor standing by a bedside. He wrote to his host, that same evening, asking if anything unexpected had happened, but a letter crossed his inquiry, telling him that the youngest daughter had been taken ill just after his departure. The child was very fond of him, and this was obviously a case of thought transference.

As a rough guide it is safe to assume that any perfectly natural action or event, when the dreamer merely looks on but does not take any active part, as seen in a dream, is a warning or a mirage from some outside source. On the other hand, where the dreamer visualises himself, or herself, as one of the actors in the mimic drama, the message comes from within, and should be interpreted as affecting the dreamer personally.

But in both cases the action or event must be a reasonable one—something that *could* happen in everyday life, though it might appear extremely improbable as far as the dreamer is concerned. Thus, if we dream of flying upon wings, or without any physical means of support, it is not a Vision, though it may be a Dream. But if you are flying in an aeroplane, the case is altered, as that is a possibility, though you may, personally, dread such an attempt, and know that you would never make such a journey.

These points are very important, because all impossible actions and events should be put down to some physical cause, first of all, and should only be treated as bona fide dreams when no other explanation appears possible.

Not only is dreaming almost universal to-day, but we are forced to assume that it has always held a prominent place in human history. Naturally there are not many records of the dreams of our early ancestors, as it used to be a long and laborious process to make a permanent record of any event, however important it might be. But the Bible contains many instances of these Visions, and in most cases they came as warnings of some impending event.

But of recent years all this has been changed, and many well-known professional people—particularly doctors and scientists—have written books in which they have recorded authentic cases that have come under their notice. Strangely enough, there are many cases of people who have received, in sleep, a perfectly accurate Vision of some actual place—a town or a house, for instance—that they have never seen, yet, later on, every detail has proved correct.

An author had a vivid dream of a visit to Eastbourne— a popular resort about which he knew nothing whatever. He saw himself driven from the railway station to an hotel on the front ; then he watched the incoming tide for some time before turning down a street off the front in order to have a cup of coffee at a café where he knew they made excellent coffee.

The dream was so vivid that he even saw the name of the street—Queen Street or some such common name. Yet he had never been to Eastbourne in his life. So impressed was he by the reality of his dream that he determined to " make it come true ! "

At the first opportunity he made the journey, went straight to the hotel, which he recognised readily, and then turned down Queen Street, where he found the identical café at the first corner on the left !

This type of dream is by no means uncommon, and it is very difficult to find an explanation. Obviously it is not a warning, either of good or evil—it is merely a peculiar experience, and raises the question whether, in very deep sleep, the spirit or mentality can ignore physical space. Some casual reference to Eastbourne, perhaps in a newspaper paragraph, may have raised a subconscious thought that he had never been there, and then, in sleep, he visited the town mentally.

A somewhat similar experience, though not a dream, happened to a man who was an enthusiastic gardener. One Saturday, he devoted the whole day to building a rockery in a shady corner of his garden, and worked till it was too dark to see. When he was tidying up before the evening meal, he found, to his horror, that a very valuable emerald stud was missing from the front of his shirt!

It was far too dark to go out again, so all he could do was to go to bed as usual, and wait. But as soon as he was dressed next morning, he went straight to a certain spot on the rockery, and there saw the stud lying on the surface of the soil. How did he know— for he went straight to the spot, feeling certain that the stud was there? Many investigators would say that his mentality had been searching the rockery while his body was asleep, and probably they would be correct.

It may be asked why certain interpretations are attached to certain dreams, but this point is really a simple one when understood. It is impossible to conceive a Thought without some article, action, or quality associated with it. You cannot actually dream a warning of danger, but you can and do dream some mental picture that is associated in your mind with a sense of danger. Dreams, therefore, are mental pictures of some thought of your own, or a message from some other person, conveyed to you in the form of a pictured incident.

Many people believe that dreams go by contrary, but this is far from being the case, though it is true in certain instances. Many people, ancient and modern, have studied this question, and, as was only natural, in certain cases their interpretations differ greatly.

Much of our knowledge concerning Dreams comes to us from the East, and from sources that are many centuries old ; but it would not be accurate for the West to accept all these, as certain articles would not have the same association among people of such different mentality.

The Peacock, in the East, was a sacred bird, and it meant death for anyone other than a Priest to possess even a feather—hence the popular and very prevalent association of ill-luck with a Peacock feather. But in the West we have never run any risk of losing our lives in this way, so the old interpretation cannot stand.

The various readings given in this book are intended for modern use, by Western people, and where much doubt exists, the various meanings are included or the particular dream symbol is omitted altogether.

THE INTERPRETATIONS OF DREAMS

Arranged in Alphabetical Order

A

ABANDON.—This is an unfavourable dream, and indicates the loss of friends, or the failure of some fortunate expectation. Trouble is indicated, whether you Abandon some other person, or whether they Abandon you.

ABBESS.—To dream that you meet an Abbess is a favourable sign, showing restored peace and comfort after some distress or illness. See also **NUN.**

ABBEY.—Anything connected with a church shows peace of mind and freedom from anxiety. The more important the structure, the better the prospect.

ABBOT.—It is a warning of ill-health if you meet an Abbot in your dream; but there is comfort behind it, for you will recover in due course. See also **BISHOP.**

ABDICATE.—To dream of a monarch Abdicating his throne in any kingdom denotes anarchy and revolution there.

ABDOMEN.—It is an omen of contrary, when you are in pain in your dream; your health will be good, and your affairs will prosper because of your physical vigour. But if you dream of your unclothed Abdomen, then it is an unfortunate omen, especially for lovers or married people, for you may expect unfaithfulness or even treachery on the part of some loved person. Do not rashly give your confidence after such a dream.

ABDUCTED.—To dream of being carried off by force means that you will carry out your plans against all opposition.

ABHORRENCE.—To dream that you dislike anything or any person is an omen that depends on the circumstances. If your feeling of distaste disturbs you seriously, then it foretells difficulties in your path ; but if you merely dislike any article, and can get rid of it, then you will overcome your worries.

ABJECT.—To dream of feeling abject presages hard times, but only for a little while.

ABODE.—Strange houses show that your affairs are in an unsettled condition. If, in your dream, you go into a strange house, you will probably venture on some new undertaking before long. If you are refused admission, or find that you cannot get in, then be careful in your plans and avoid needless risk.

ABORTION.—A warning as regards health or the happiness of your partner in marriage ; be on your guard as to both.

ABOVE (Hanging and about to fall).—Some danger awaits you, but may be avoided if the object does not fall.

ABROAD.—A change of work is probable. This dream shows that you are in an unsettled state of mind.

ABSCESS.—A dream of illness is one of contrary meaning, and signifies that you will enjoy good health, or a speedy recovery if you are already ill.

ABSCOND.—To dream that some person, whether stranger or acquaintance, has absconded with his employer's money, or otherwise done some serious wrong, is a warning to you of treachery among those around you. If you yourself are the person in question, the injury will be slight, and you will recover from your losses.

ABSENCE.—This is usually a dream of contrary. If you dream of the death of an absent friend, it foretells a wedding. See **ABROAD**.

ABSINTHE.—Drinking spirits or cocktails in your dream is a warning of coming trouble ; the more you drink, the more serious the disaster will be.

ABSTINENCE.—To dream that you refuse to drink is a sign of good fortune coming, but it may not be lasting in its effects.

ABUNDANCE.—To dream of plenty is always a good sign, and indicates success in your plans.

ABUSE.—To dream that someone is abusing you is a bad sign, but it applies to your business affairs only. But to dream that you are abusing some other person foretells success, after hard work. See **ACCUSE.**

ABYSS.—To dream of any hollow space is a sign of difficulties ahead ; it is an obstacle dream. If you escape from the Abyss, you will overcome your troubles, but if you fall therein, then be careful in your business affairs. Do not lend money, for it will not be returned to you.

ACACIA.—If in season, disappointment ; but to dream of this flower in winter is a sign of tender hopes which will be realised.

ACADEMY.—To dream that you are master or mistress of an Academy, indicates that you will be reduced in your circumstances ; if single, that your intended marriage will be characterised by adversity.

ACCENT.—To dream of hearing speech in strange Accents or a foreign tongue presages hasty news and a long journey.

ACCEPTED.—To dream that you have been accepted by your lover, or if a woman, that your lover has proposed to you and that you have accepted him, is generally considered a dream of contrary. It is a warning that your love affairs will not prosper, or at least that it will be a long time coming right. In some localities, however, it is looked upon as a fortunate omen.

ACCIDENT.—This dream depends entirely upon the surroundings. If the Accident occurs at sea, it means disappointment in your love affairs. But if it happens on land, it concerns your personal or business ventures. See also **BOAT, CARRIAGE, WAGON.**

ACCOUNTS.—To dream that you are engaged in adding up Accounts, or checking business figures, is a warning to you to be careful, or you will lose money by giving credit too freely.

ACCUSE.—Obviously, there is not much difference between this and **ABUSE,** except that the nature of the trouble is more clearly defined. It is a sign of approaching trouble in business, but in this case, if you can prove your innocence, it shows that you will overcome your difficulties. Vague abuse will show undefined troubles or worries, whereas a definite accusation indicates a more serious matter, some special trouble.

ACE (In Cards).—Diamonds—quarrels ; Hearts—News ; Spades—Bad luck ; Clubs—Money.

ACHE.—This depends entirely upon the circumstances, but it is usually found to be a case of contrary meaning. If it is a trivial Ache, it is probably due to some physical cause, and would be a sign of ill-health. But if the pain is severe and obviously imaginary, it denotes some important event that will prove beneficial to you. To the business man, it foretells good trade, a fortunate season's business. To the lover, it indicates a favourable time for him to push his suit. To the farmer, it promises a good and profitable harvest, with high prices. To the sailor, it shows a successful voyage. See **ILLNESS.**

ACID.—To dream of handling Acids, foretells danger concerning a promise. Fulfill your own promises and do not trust blindly in those of others.

ACORN.—As a rule, any indication of Nature's goodwill is a favourable sign. See also such omens as **CORN-FIELD, FLOWERS, HARVEST, HEDGES, TREES.** To the lover, it is a sign of future happiness ; to those in difficulties, a proof of speedy relief. If you gather the Acorns in your dream, it is supposed to indicate a legacy, or some good fortune from outside your own life.

ACQUAINTANCE.—To dream of some person whom you know is a good sign, but it depends upon the degree of friendship, and also upon what happens in your dream. If you quarrel, it is a bad sign, and often applies to the health of the dreamer. See such omens as **ABUSE** or **ACCUSE**.

ACQUITTED.—To dream of being accused before a court and Acquitted foretells prosperity to yourself and failure to your enemies.

ACROBAT.—To watch other people performing clever gymnastic feats is a dream of contrary ; be careful or an accident will befall you. Do not take long journeys for seven days after such a dream. If the Acrobat in your dream has an accident, or is unable to perform the attempted feat, then you will escape the full results of the peril that is hanging over you.

ACROSTIC.—Puzzles of almost every sort, when appearing in a dream, are a warning of coming trouble, probably caused by some hasty decision of your own. Postpone new ventures and take no unusual business risk.

ACTING.—To dream that you are Acting, or taking part in some entertainment, is a warning that some slight difficulty will delay the consummation of your plans. Persevere, however, for all will come right.

ACTOR OR ACTRESS.—To dream that you meet an Actor or Actress is an indication of trouble of a domestic character. Keep your temper, and do not allow yourself to be disturbed if anything goes wrong at home.

ADAM.—It is claimed to be a fortunate omen if you dream that you see either of our first parents, Adam or Eve. If you speak to them, or if they speak to you, it indicates some delay in the realisation of your wishes, but you must be patient. To see both Adam and Eve at once is the most fortunate dream you can have.

ADDER.—Beware of false friends when you dream of a snake or a serpent. In some districts, it is held to mean the breaking off of a valued friendship, perhaps by death.

ADDRESS.—If you dream of writing the address, be careful of your financial affairs, and do not enter into risky speculations.

ADIEU.—To dream that you are saying good-bye to anyone is an indication of misfortune due to ill-health. Take no risks, such as chills.

ADJUTANT.—To dream that you are in the company of an officer of the army is a sign of new friendship. The higher the rank of the officer, the more advantageous to yourself the friendship will prove.

ADMIRAL.—To dream of a naval officer of high rank, foretells events of importance to yourself.

ADMIRE.—If you dream that you yourself are Admired, it indicates useful friendships with people whom you like—it is, in that sense, a dream of contrary. If, however, you find yourself Admiring some other person, it shows the friendly feeling of some other person for you, but this may not be the person about whom you are dreaming. This point should be borne in mind, as it is very apt to mislead.

ADOPTED OR ADOPTION.—This is a dream of contrary. If you dream that you have been Adopted by some one, or that you have Adopted some child, it shows that some relation or close friend will appeal to you for help in some crisis.

ADORNMENT.—To dream that you have received a present of some article of clothing, such as a frock or a hat, is a dream of contrary. Expect some misfortune shortly. The more elaborate or costly the gift, the greater the coming trouble. But if, in your dream, you refuse the present, then you will overcome your trouble. If you accept, but do not actually wear the gift, then expect difficulties that will require great care and patience on your part.

ADRIFT.—To dream that you are Adrift in a boat is a warning of difficulty ahead—it is an obstacle dream. If you reach land safely, you will overcome your troubles, but if you fall out of the boat, or if the boat should be upset by rough waves, then expect very serious difficulties. Even then you may swim to land, or be rescued, which would indicate ultimate success.

ADULTERY.—To dream of temptation to crime means a virtuous life and success to your plans ; to dream of guilt forebodes failure.

ADVANCEMENT.—This is a most favourable sign, and indicates success in some important undertaking. You may be your own master, yet if you dream that you are in some employment and are Advanced, your success is certain. This dream often occurs in connection with legal matters. But if you dream of the lawsuit itself, you will lose.

ADVENTURES.—To meet with exciting Adventures in a dream predicts a surprising alteration in your fortune.

ADVERSARY.—A dream of contrary meaning. It is always a good sign if you dream of an opponent or some business or professional rival. It indicates difficulties in the immediate future, but you will overcome these if you are in earnest.

ADVERSITY.—This omen has much the same meaning as **ADVERSARY**—it is a favourable dream and indicates prosperity.

ADVERTISEMENT.—To dream that you are Advertising in the papers is a sign of difficulties ahead of you. It is a good sign, on the other hand, to read an Advertisement inserted by someone else.

ADVICE.—An indication of useful friendships, whether you are being Advised, or whether you are Advising some other person. In this case the dream person concerned is seldom the same as the actual friend—you must seek elsewhere for the real name.

ADVOCATE.—To dream that you are a solicitor is a good omen and foretells success. If you are a barrister in your dream, then there will be a longer delay, but success is certain, unless, in Court, you dream that you lose your case.

AEROPLANE.—A sign that money is coming to you,

but your methods may not be above suspicion. Study your plans carefully.

AFFECTION.—To dream that there is great Affection shown between you and some other person is a dream of contrary. It shows that you are not quite straight in some of your plans.

AFFIANCED.—This dream depends upon the person to whom you appear to be engaged. If he, or she, is beautiful, strong, or well-made, it is not a good sign. If the fiancé is plain and quiet, then all is well for the future.

AFFILIATION.—An omen of a powerful enemy. Be cautious.

AFFLICTION.—A dream of contrary—the greater your trouble and difficulty in your dream, the more certain is your success in life.

AFFLUENCE.—The greater your appearance of show and wealth in a dream, the heavier will be your loss in business, for this is an omen of contrary.

AFFRONT.—To dream that you feel offended by the conduct of some person is a dream of contrary, unless you quarrel violently and part in anger. To dream that you annoy someone else is a sign of trouble in the near future.

AFLOAT.—On smooth water, a happy destiny is in view ; on a rough sea, troubles not of your own making.

AFRAID.—Another dream of contrary, since it shows that you realise your difficulties, and are likely to overcome them To the timid lover, it foretells success.

AFRICA.—An unexpected advancement in your fortunes will soon take place.

AFTERNOON.—A fine afternoon warns the dreamer to act cautiously in personal affairs. Fortune favours you if you beware of knavery from those around you.

AGE.—To worry about your own age, when dreaming, is a bad sign, and indicates an approaching illness. In a sense, it can be looked upon as due to physical causes rather than as a dream warning. The more you worry, the more serious the coming illness will be.

AGED PEOPLE.—It is always a fortunate omen when you dream of old people, either men or women. The more of them you see, the more fortunate your dream. If they are in rags, it indicates difficulties, but if you tackle your problems boldly, you will pull through.

AGONY.—Authorities differ over this dream, and it might be wise to treat it as an obstacle dream. Some people claim that to feel pain in your dream is a very fortunate sign for business affairs. Others say that it shows domestic troubles. Sometimes both versions might prove true, if a married man, or an affianced lover, gave over-much time to business and neglected his wife and family.

AGREEMENT OR BUSINESS DOCUMENT.—This dream is always held to be a warning of some flaw in your plans, some oversight that will upset your calculations and hopes. If you do not actually sign the agreement, but only read it, you will get through all right.

AGUE.—As with most dreams of bodily pain, this is a fortunate omen.

AIR.—A dream about the open air depends entirely upon the circumstances. If the air is clear and the sky is blue, then it indicates success. But if the air is misty or foggy, or if there are clouds about, then trouble is foretold, and you should postpone, or reconsider any proposed change.

AIR-GUN.—To have one given you, means an enemy. To fire it, is a warning to postpone decisions for a day or two.

AIRSHIP.—A sign of money making, but watch your speculations, or you may be caught, and lose instead of gain.

AISLE.—The inside of a church, when forming part of a dream, is considered unfortunate.

ALDERMEN.—To dream that you are in the company of civic authorities, such as the Mayor and Aldermen, is an omen of warning. Be careful of your speculations and of your conduct generally.

ALEHOUSE.—Not at all a good omen to find yourself inside an inn or public-house. If you keep outside the premises, you will spare yourself much worry.

ALLIGATOR OR CROCODILE.—To dream of any unusual animal denotes an enemy, and you should be cautious in speculations or in making new business ventures.

ALMONDS.—This is one of the unreliable omens, since it is looked upon as favourable in the East, whereas in the West, the authorities differ. If you are eating the Almonds, and enjoy them, you can look upon it as a good sign, but if the nuts are bitter to the taste, then you should be careful, for your ventures are liable to fail. Should you dream of the **ALMOND TREE,** and not of the fruit, it is a good sign, both in your home and in your business.

ALMS.—This dream depends upon the circumstances. If in your dream, some one begs of you, and you refuse, it is a sign of misfortune for the dreamer. But if you give, and give freely, then it is a sign of great happiness, either to yourself, or to some intimate friend.

ALBATROSS.—An introduction to a stranger who will tell good news.

ALMANAC.—To dream you are reading one, a slight quarrel with someone dear to you.

ALPACA.—To dream of the material means a lucky find ; of the animal, a valuable gift will be received.

AMBER.—To see Amber is a warning against pride, which may be a barrier between you and someone you love.

AMBULANCE.—This means speedy realisation of your desire.

ALIEN.—To dream that you are an Alien denotes friendship and love.

ALOE.—To dream of Aloe trees, denotes bad tidings.

ALPHABET.—The return of an absent friend.

ALUM.—One beneath you has a bitterness of mind and tongue against you.

ALTAR.—To dream you are inside a church is not considered fortunate ; it does not carry the same fortunate meaning as a view of the outside of the sacred building.

AMERICA.—A good fortune is coming to you through your own efforts.

AMMONIA.—Danger through illness or accidents ; take no risks for a time.

AMOROUS.—If you dream you are of an Amorous disposition it is a sign that you are likely to be the victim of scandal.

AMULET.—To dream you are wearing one means that you have an important decision to make shortly. Think well before choosing.

ANARCHIST.—A warning as to financial caution, especially if you dream of seeing more than one.

ANCESTORS.—To dream of your relations, earlier in period than your father or mother, is considered a warning of illness.

ANCHOR.—If seen clearly, this is a fortunate sight, but the whole of the anchor should be visible to the dreamer. If it is actually in the water, it indicates disappointment.

ANECDOTE.—A pleasant dream denoting social success.

ANGELS.—Another fortunate dream, but it refers particularly to love affairs and friendships.

ANGER.—A dream of contrary. If you are angry in your dream with some person whom you know, it shows that you will benefit in some way through that person. If it is a stranger, then some unexpected good news will reach you.

ANGLING.—As with **ANCHOR,** when seen in the water, this dream indicates disappointment in some cherished project.

ANIMALS.—To see wild Animals in a dream is generally a dream of contrary ; but there are a few special Animals such as **LION, LEOPARD, TIGER,** which carry distinct meanings. Any very unusual creature, such as a crocodile, is a bad sign. Domestic Animals have separate meanings, and the **CAT** and **DOG** are not considered good dream omens. Cows and Bulls depend upon their attitude ; if they are peaceful, they are a good omen ; but if they attack you, then expect difficulties in your business ventures.

ANKLE.—An injury to your foot or Ankle in a dream is a fortunate omen, but you will have to face difficulties for some time first.

ANNOY.—To dream that you are Annoyed about something is a dream of contrary—good fortune awaits your plans.

ANTHEM.—Church music is naturally associated with the interior of the building, and is not, therefore, very favourable. But the combination of pleasant musical sounds with an unfavourable omen will indicate illness in your family circle.

ANTS.—To dream of these industrious little creatures shows business activity, but in some fresh district or surrounding.

ANT-EATER.—An unfortunate dream. Take no risks.

ANTELOPE.—To dream you see one means that someone dear to you has placed faith and affection upon you.

ANVIL.—This is generally considered a good omen, but there should not be much noise connected with the dream.

ANXIETY.—A dream of contrary, which shows that some worry will be relieved very shortly.

APE.—As in the case of all unusual animals seen in dreams, this is a warning of coming trouble.

APOLOGY.—A change of companionship ; possibly a return to a former friendship.

APPAREL.—It is a dream of contrary to be concerned over your clothes. The newer and more up-to-date your attire, the greater the trouble coming across your path. To see yourself in rags is, therefore, a very fortunate sign. But the true meaning of a dream concerning clothes often depends upon the **COLOUR**, which you should consult. If you see yourself or other people in a dream without clothes, it is a sign of some unexpected good fortune.

APPARITION.—No harm is foretold by a dream of ghosts or other Apparitions, unless their presence or sudden appearance frightens you or makes you ill. In that case, you must expect financial difficulties, perhaps ill-health.

APPETITE.—It is not a good sign when you appear to be hungry in your dream; it is Nature's warning of some health trouble. Mere feasting is also a bad sign, but refers to money matters.

APPLAUSE.—To dream that you receive the open approval of your friends and neighbours is an omen of contrary. Beware of family quarrels or separation from some friend, due to ill feeling.

APPLES.—Fruit is generally a good omen in a dream, as with all products of Nature; but if you eat the fruit, you will yourself be responsible for some misfortune. To dream of an **APPLE TREE** is also fortunate.

APRICOT.—To dream of this popular fruit is a sign of coming prosperity, both in business matters and love affairs.

APRON.—It is an omen of contrary when you dream of any mishap to your clothes. If you tear your apron, it means some small benefit, as the garment is not an important one.

APRIL FOOL.—To dream that you are made one means that you will soon be given power over another; be careful to use it well.

AQUAMARINE.—To dream of this jewel assures you of the affection of a very youthful relative or friend.

ARAB.—To dream of a foreign person concerns your love affairs, or some important transaction, with someone quite outside your family and usual business circle.

ARBOUR.—To see one in a dream means that you will hear secrets; to be in one, that your own secrets will be revealed.

ARCH.—It is not a good sign to dream of passing under an Arch, since it foretells interference in your love affairs.

It is, in reality, a mild form of obstacle dream, that concerns your personal affairs, rather than financial.

ARCHER.—To the single, a speedy engagement. If already married, be true ; danger is near you.

ARENA.—A warning of danger. Avoid crowds. If not alone in your dream the danger is lessened.

ARK.—An excellent dream denoting safety and protection for you.

ARM.—To dream of an accident to your Arm is a sign of ill-health in the family circle. To lose one Arm generally foretells death, or a long and serious illness. To dream of a stiff Arm is usually a sign of some money loss, due to ill-health.

ARMED MEN OR ARMY.—An obstacle dream, but it only foretells difficulty, or a journey, followed by a successful issue of your venture. If the men are fighting, it becomes a serious matter.

ARMCHAIR.—Hasty news.

ARMISTICE.—This presages promotion in business.

ARREST.—A sudden and unexpected success will come to you, but choose your friends carefully.

ARSON.—Not a fortunate dream. News of accidents at sea ; possibly to yourself.

ARTERY.—This denotes a message to the healthy. To the sick, slow recovery.

ARTICHOKES.—Vexations and troubles which, however, you will surmount.

ASPS.—This portends enemies and if you are stung your enemies will do you harm ; but if you kill the Asps you will triumph.

ARROW.—To dream that you have been struck by an Arrow, is a sign of misfortune from some unexpected source. Some person who appears to be friendly is really working against your interests.

ARTIST.—To dream that you are acting as model for your portrait is a warning of treachery on the part of some acquaintance. If, however, you dream that you are painting the portrait of someone, then your plans should be revised carefully, for you will risk failure by striving to take an unfair advantage.

ASCEND.—Any form of progress upwards is a sign of success, and if you appear to reach the top of a **HILL,** it shows that you will have great success.

ASHES.—Something lost through your own carelessness.

ASPARAGUS.—Another valuable gift from Mother Nature—a favourable sign. Push on with your plans, for you will be successful.

ASSAULT.—False information will be given you. Be on your guard and prove the facts.

ASS OR DONKEY.—If you ride a Donkey in your dream, it is a good sign for your love affairs, unless you experience trouble or difficulty with the animal. To see the Donkey, without riding it, is generally accepted as a sign of some senseless quarrel which is not to your credit. If the animal kicks you, you can safely conclude that you will deserve all the misfortune that may follow the quarrel.

ASTHMA.—A warning to you that some favourite scheme will not prove as profitable as you expect. Revise your plans, and avoid all speculation or risk.

ASTERS.—A sign of pleasant happenings soon to come.

ASYLUM.—This suggestive omen depends, for its correct interpretation, upon the circumstances of the dream. If you remain outside the building, you should take every chance of helping those in trouble, when you may expect good fortune for yourself. But if you find yourself inside, then look out for trouble of a serious nature.

ATHLETE.—Not a good dream to any but the very strong ; beware of overstrain.

ATLAS.—To dream that you are consulting a map or an Atlas is considered a sign of business ventures at a distance ; in the case of the Atlas, it probably indicates a visit abroad.

ATMOSPHERE.—Blue skies and sunshine form one of the most fortunate of all dreams, since it foretells prosperity in money matters, happiness in domestic affairs, and the company of faithful friends. But clouds, rain, or thunderstorms are all signs of trouble and misfortune. to be read according to their severity. It is less serious to witness a storm than to be at its mercy.

ATTENDANT.—A speedy rise in position.

ATTIC.—A premonition of an engagement to the single. If married avoid flirtation.

ATTORNEY.—Business worries are in front of you. Be careful of your plans and avoid all speculation in stocks and shares.

AUCTION.—An unfavourable sign, somewhat similar in meaning to **ATTORNEY** or **LAWYER.** Be careful, or some acquaintance will take advantage of you. Do not lend money.

AUDIENCE.—Social pleasures and distinctions to come.

AUGUST.—To dream of summer in winter time foretells unexpected news.

AUNT.—To dream of close relations is a fortunate sign, and shows success in money matters. See also such words as **FATHER, MOTHER, UNCLE, ANCESTOR.**

AUTHOR.—To dream of a great Author brings unexpected pleasures to the single. To the married, good fortune in the family.

AUTOMATON.—A peculiar turn of events will soon surprise you.

AUTUMN.—There are unfortunate and hostile influences around you. Walk warily and you may avoid them.

AVALANCHE.—Good fortune of an astonishing nature will soon befall you.

AWL.—Increased prosperity, but not through your own efforts.

AXE.—A warning of danger which only your own forethought and bravery can avert.

AWAKEN.—It is a good omen if you Awaken some person in the course of your dream, and it will go far to soften any unfavourable omen that may be present. This is especially the case if the sleeper is in bed, as the colour **WHITE** then helps the good fortune, and serves to confirm the fortunate issue of events.

B

BABY.—It is a curious fact that it is fortunate to see **CHILDREN** in a dream, if they are old enough to be independent, but a helpless baby is a bad sign. It usually shows some disappointment in love, or if the baby is unwell, a serious illness or even death in the family. See **CHILDREN**.

BACCHUS.—A sign of hardworking days to come.

BACHELOR.—If the man is young, it is a good sign, but if old, the dream foreshadows loneliness, or the loss of a friend.

BACK.—If in your dream some person turns his or her Back upon you, it shows opposition and difficulty, though this may not be very serious or persistent. If the person turns round and faces you, it is a sign that all will come well again before long. To dream of your own Back is a favourable sign, though this is not met so often as dreams of your arms or legs or body.

BACK-DOOR.—To dream that you are making use of the Back-door instead of the front entrance of your house is a warning of some coming change in your fortunes. This may be for good or for evil, according to the other circumstances.

BACON.—An unfortunate omen, whatever happens in the dream, whether you are eating it or merely buying it. Generally it concerns the health.

BACKGAMMON.—To dream of taking part in it, a test of your character is soon to be made.

BADGE.—You are under observation and will shortly be promoted.

BADGER.—A typical dream showing that hard work is in front of you.

BAG.—A sign of better times, especially if a heavy one.

BAGPIPES.—As with the most unusual things, when seen in a dream, this musical instrument is not a favourable sign, and in particular it indicates matrimonial worry and difficulty.

BAILIFF.—To dream that you have trouble with this officer of the Court is an omen of contrary—some unexpected legacy will come your way before long.

BAIT.—Do not trust blindly in those who seek to please you.

BAIZE.—Exciting times to come. Keep a cool head.

BAKER AND BAKING.—To dream of some person Baking is a good sign in every way; you will not have to wait long for some favourable turn of events. But if you yourself are Baking, it indicates the serious illness of some one dear to you—either a member of your family, or your betrothed, if you happen to be engaged.

BALCONY.—This dream should be classed among the obstacle omens, though the difficulty to be faced will not be a serious one. If you leave the balcony, all will be well. It is slightly more serious if you are seated than if you are standing, as your quick recovery is delayed.

BALD.—A dream concerning your health—the less hair you appear to have, the more serious will be the coming illness. In the case of a woman, it indicates money troubles, or some difficult love affair.

BALE.—Good fortune, more or less, according to whether it is cotton or wool.

BALLAD.—To hear one, beware of false judgments; to sing one, someone you care for thinks you unkind.

BALL.—This dream depends upon the circumstances. If you see yourself among the dancers, some favourable news will reach you. But to watch other people dancing and enjoying themselves shows that some cherished wish will fail to realise.

BALLAST.—Look to your associates; one is not a true friend.

BALLET.—To dream of a stage Ballet, or other professional dancing, is a warning concerning your health. Take no risks if the weather is wet or stormy.

BALLOON.—Another unusual omen, and therefore an unfavourable sign for the dreamer.

BALLOT.—A difference in position and surroundings possibly for the better.

BALM.—True friendship is near you.

BALUSTRADE.—News of accidents on river or ocean, possibly for yourself.

BANANA.—A fortunate omen, though the dream may concern some small affair only.

BANDAGE.—Fresh influences will surround you.

BANDY.—To dream that your legs have become deformed is a sign of contrary—good fortune awaits you.

BANISHMENT.—If in your dream you are forced to leave your abode it is a fortunate sign. The more serious the disturbance appears to be, the greater your future prosperity.

BANK OR BANKING.—To dream that you have dealings with a Bank is a bad sign, because it indicates some sudden loss of money.

BANKRUPTCY.—To dream that you have lost money and are now Bankrupt should be taken as a warning. Some plan is not very creditable to you and should be abandoned at once, as trouble will follow. Be cautious in your transactions and seek the advice of friends older than yourself.

BANNER OR FLAG.—A good omen, but it concerns your personal position rather than your business affairs.

BANNS.—Although this dream concerns the interior of a church, which is not considered fortunate, you can rely upon some good fortune following an unpleasant experience.

BANQUET.—This is usually considered a fortunate omen if the dreamer is young, but not if he or she is old.

BANTAM COCK.—An unwise plan which may succeed but will not satisfy you.

BAPTISM.—This foretells disappointment through unforeseen circumstances.

BAR.—Your friends esteem you more highly than you know.

BARBER.—To dream that you are in a Barber's shop foretells some difficulty in your business affairs.

BARGAIN.—A warning to be steadfast and trust your own opinions.

BARGE.—You are about to travel some distance. Be careful.

BASKET.—An obstacle dream, since it is so easy to upset the contents. Be careful of your business ventures or you will lose money.

BAT.—Treachery is clearly shown when you dream about these curious nocturnal creatures. Beware of discussing your plans. Do not lend money and avoid all speculation.

BARE FEET.—It is considered fortunate to dream that you are naked. If only the feet are bare, then you may expect some trouble or difficulty, but by perseverance and hard work you will prove successful.

BARLEY.—A good omen, as with most things connected with Nature.

BARMAID.—To dream of a Barmaid is a sign of difficulty, probably due to your own carelessness. See **INN**.

BARN.—This is a favourable dream if the Barn is full, or nearly so ; but it is unfortunate to see an empty Barn, with open doors.

BARRACKS.—Your difficulties will soon be lessened.

BARREL.—An upright and full, prosperity ; if rolling and empty, hard times to come.

BASHFUL.—A happy time at a large party.

BASIN.—To dream that you are eating or drinking from a Basin is an unnatural dream—if you are in love, you must expect difficulty, and may not marry the first object of your affections.

BATH AND BATHING.—The meaning of this dream depends entirely upon what is happening. If it is in the open and the water is clear, then it shows success in business. But if the water is dirty, or muddy, or choked with weeds, then you may expect difficulty and trouble in your work or profession. If you are yourself taking a Bath indoors, it is not a good sign. If the water is cold, it shows sorrow ; if hot, then separation from some friend or loved one, perhaps a quarrel if steam is seen. To see yourself naked is a good sign in itself, but you must not be in water. See **CLOTHES.**

BATTLE.—This is another unusual event, and foretells trouble ; a serious quarrel with neighbours or lover. But if you are on the winning side, whether fighting alone or with others, then things will come right in the end.

BAYONET.—A quarrel soon to be made up.

BAZAAR.—To dream that you are assisting at a Bazaar, or any other cause devoted to charity, is a fortunate omen for your love affairs.

BEANS.—Difficulties lie ahead of you, be careful.

BEAR.—An indication of difficulties ahead of you, but that they are within your power, if you work earnestly. If you succeed in killing the Bear, or driving it away, you may expect success eventually.

BEARD.—If you see, in your dream, some person with a full Beard, you may expect some unexpected success. The fuller the Beard the better for the dreamer.

BEASTS.—Most animals represent difficulties and trouble, when seen in a dream, unless in some manner you drive them away. Even our domestic pets, cats and dogs, are not fortunate. But birds, as a rule, form a good omen. See **CATS, DOGS, BIRDS, CANARY, DOVE, PEACOCK, PIGEON, etc.**

BEACON.—Avoid misunderstandings, but should you unavoidably quarrel, take the first step towards reconciliation, or you will regret it.

BEADS.—False friends or dissatisfaction.

BEAM.—If of wood, a burden to be borne ; if of light, a well-merited reward.

BEATING.—If a married man dreams that he is Beating

his wife, it is a very fortunate sign and denotes married happiness and a comfortable home. But for lovers, it is considered a bad dream. It is also fortunate if a man dreams that he is Beating some woman who is not his wife. In the same way, if a father or mother dreams that they are punishing one of their own children, it is a fortunate sign, but not if the child is a stranger.

BEAUTY.—A dream of contrary. If you see yourself as Beautiful, it indicates an illness ; if some other person, then they will be the invalids.

BED.—To dream that you are in a strange Bed shows some unexpected good turn in your business affairs ; if you are in your own Bed, it concerns your love affairs. To dream of making a Bed, is a sign of a change of residence. To sit on a Bed is considered a sign of an early marriage.

BED-CLOTHES.—This may be considered a dream of contrary. If wealthy people dream of plenty of Bed-clothes, it is a warning of loss of money. But if the dreamer is poor, or only moderately well-to-do, then it is a sign of coming improvement in the financial condition.

BEDROOM.—If the Bedroom in your dream is more sumptuous than your own, it shows a change in your circumstances that will eventually prove favourable for you. But you must be prepared for some delay if your dream concerns the earlier hours of the night ; whereas the change will come soon, if your dream is of the dawn, or of the early morning hours.

BEEF.—To dream that you are eating Beef or Mutton, shows that you will remain comfortably well off, but will never be rich. But if you appear to have plenty of food, but are unable to eat it, then you will have to appeal to others to help you.

BEER.—If you dream that you are drinking Beer or Ale, it is a sign of some monetary loss in connection with speculation. If you only see the Ale or Beer, or if other people are drinking it, but not yourself, the loss will be small. For all that, you should be careful in betting or speculating.

BEES.—This is a good omen unless they sting you in your dream. They concern business matters, however, not love or friendship.

BEETLES.—To dream of these unpleasant little creatures is a sign of quarrelling with your friends or some difficulty in your affairs due to malice. If you kill the insects, you will put matters right quickly.

BEETROOT.—Some interference with your love affairs is indicated when you dream of Beetroot; but all will go well if you eat it.

BEGGAR.—A sign that you will receive unexpected help —a dream of contrary.

BELFRY.—Good tidings from a distance.

BELLE OF THE BALL.—To dream that you are dancing with the prettiest woman in the room, is an omen of contrary—you may expect trouble in your family affairs, or from some woman acquaintance. If a woman dreams that she is the Belle of the Ball, it has a similar meaning, provided she is dancing. But if she finds herself neglected, then the trouble will be short-lived and all will end happily.

BELLOWS.—It is considered very unfortunate to dream that you are using the Bellows on the fire, for you will soon be confronted by difficulties due to your own actions.

BELLS.—To dream that you hear the ringing of Bells is a sign of coming news, but it may not be favourable.

BELT.—To dream of putting one on is a good omen of a happy future.

BENCH.—An unfortunate dream; attend carefully to work, or you may lose it.

BEQUEST.—To dream that you are bequeathing money or property to other people is an omen of contrary— you will receive money from some unexpected source.

BEREAVEMENT.—News of a friend's marriage soon to take place.

BERRIES.—Social activities of a happy nature. If you dream you are picking many blackberries, financial gains.

BEST MAN.—To dream you are acting as best man denotes the failure of a plan of yours through a false friend.

BET.—To dream that you are Betting, do not trust your own opinions too much. To see others Betting, do not allow other people's opinions to interfere with you.

BETROTHED.—It is not a favourable sign to dream that you have just become engaged to be married—expect trouble among your family circle, or with your lover if you are really engaged.

BICYCLE.—To dream that you are riding one means that you will have to make an important decision. Think well, and then act as *you* think best.

BIER.—If you are lying upon it, it signifies a triumphant ending to your hopes.

BIGAMY.—Unfortunately it is considered a fortunate omen to commit Bigamy in your dreams. You are assured of a happy and prosperous married life.

BILLIARDS.—Another dream of unusual occurrence, unless you play regularly, when the omen loses all significance. It indicates some difficulty; if you are in love, or engaged, it means that you will be opposed by your betrothed's family.

BILLS.—To dream that you are paying them denotes speedy financial gains; that they are unpaid, signifies evil speaking.

BIRDS.—Usually considered to be of an uncertain nature—if you are poor and struggling. Birds indicate a coming improvement in your circumstances. But if you are wealthy, you may expect a reverse. It is a good sign if the Birds show beautiful plumage. If the Birds are singing it is always fortunate.

BIRD'S EGGS OR NEST.—If you see the Eggs in the Nest, it is a sign of money coming to you; but if the young are visible it is not a good sign.

BIRTH.—It is a good sign when a married woman dreams of giving birth to a child ; but for a single woman, it foretells trouble in the near future.

BIRTHDAY.—To dream that it is your own Birthday is a fortunate sign for money matters or business affairs. To dream that it is the Birthday of some friend or relative is a sign that they will benefit shortly, probably in connection with yourself.

BISCUITS.—A prosperous journey ; sometimes a warning of coming ill-health.

BISHOP OR CLERGYMAN.—An omen of ill-health, or some serious disappointment.

BITE.—To dream that some animal has Bitten you is a sign of trouble over your love affairs. Beware of quarrels.

BLACK.—This is an unfortunate colour when seen in a dream, unless it is in connection with a funeral, when it becomes a dream of contrary.

BLACKBERRIES.—Unlike most Nature omens, this is bad, owing to the colour. See **RASPBERRIES.**

BLACKBIRD.—Another omen that depends upon the colour. It is unfortunate.

BLANKETS.—The importance of this dream depends upon your position in life ; if you are well-to-do and dream that you are buying or receiving new Blankets, it shows that you may expect a loss of money. If you are poor, or only moderately off, then expect an improvement in your position.

BLASPHEMY.—Foretells a plan of yours will be achieved after great difficulties have been surmounted.

BLOSSOMING OF TREES.—To dream you see all sorts of trees Blossoming is a sign of joy, comfort and recreation.

BLOT.—To dream you make a Blot on a clean sheet of paper means a strange bed and some little travelling to come.

BLUNDER.—This is one of the dreams that go by " contraries " and means that you will do unexpectedly well in your next undertaking.

BLEATING OF LAMBS.—This is a very fortunate dream and indicates both prosperity in business and happiness at home. But the young Lambs must be seen with their dams, or your dream will show a disappointment at the last moment, just when you expect success.

BLEEDING.—An unfortunate omen, whatever the details of the dream ; a severe disappointment.

BLIND.—It does not matter whether you dream of Blind people, or that you yourself are Blind, it signifies treachery from someone near to you.

BLINDNESS.—To dream of Blind people, or that you yourself lose your sight is the sign of an unfortunate love affair. They say that love is Blind, and this dream supports the popular view that happiness in love affairs depends upon being Blind to the faults of the loved one.

BLOOD.—To dream of Blood in any form is an omen of severe disappointment. The exact significance would depend upon the other details of the dream, but if you yourself are bleeding anywhere, it generally indicates an unfortunate love affair, or a quarrel with some valued friend.

BLOWS.—A dream of contrary meaning. If you receive Blows in your dream, it shows a reconciliation after a quarrel, or some good fortune coming to you from a friend. To give Blows to other people is, however, a sign of trouble.

BLUE.—If you see much of this colour in your dream, it is a sign of prosperity through other people. The firm for whom you work will thrive and go ahead, so that your own financial position will improve at the same time. It may show good fortune in your love affairs, and a more comfortable and happy life owing to your marriage.

BOAR.—(To chase a wild one) unsuccessful efforts ; (to be chased) separation.

BOAT OR SHIP.—If you dream that you are sailing, and that the water is smooth, it indicates some fortunate business, or happiness in married life. If the water is rough, then you will have to face many difficulties. If you fall into the water, then your troubles will prove too much for you.

BOG.—This is not an obstacle dream, but an omen of contrary. It shows success in business or worldly affairs.

BOGEY.—To dream of a frightening apparition presages an exceedingly happy marriage.

BOLTS.—To dream that you have fastened the Bolts on the door of your room is a sign of contrary. You are longing to get away and make a fresh start elsewhere. To dream that you have been fastened in your room by some other person, is a sign of trouble ahead, largely due to your own greed or selfishness, perhaps owing to some untruth on your part. Think carefully over your conduct.

BONES OR SKELETON.—To dream of ordinary meat Bones is a sign of poverty; but if you see a human skeleton, it is a sign of property coming to you under a will.

BOOKCASE.—This is a dream of contrary, for if your Bookcase is seen almost empty in your dream, then you may expect good fortune through your own endeavours, or because of your strong personality. To dream that the Bookcase is full is a bad sign. It indicates slovenly, careless work, for which you will surely suffer, by loss of employment, or by money trouble in business.

BOOKS.—This is a good sign and indicates future happiness, though in a quiet way.

BOOTS.—You can rely upon the faithfulness of your servants or business employees, if you dream of new and comfortable boots or shoes; but if they are old or hurt your feet, you will meet with difficulties, due to your own fault. See also **SHOES.**

BORROW.—This is a bad dream, for it foretells domestic sorrow not money loss. If you dream that you repay the loan, or that someone repays you, then you will sail into smooth waters once again.

BOSOM.—To dream that your Bosom is inflamed or painful is a sign of coming illness.

BOTTLE.—This dream depends upon circumstances. If the Bottle is full, it shows prosperity; if it is empty, then misfortunes are foretold; while if you upset the contents, you may expect domestic worries.

BOUND.—To imagine yourself Bound with ropes is a dream of coming obstacles. Be careful, or trouble will overtake you.

BOUQUET.—If you retain the bunch of flowers you will be all right; but if you throw them away, or drop them, it indicates a quarrel or separation from some friend.

BOWLS.—A fortunate dream, especially if you are taking part in the game, as this denotes future prosperity.

BOW AND ARROW.—If you hit the target in your dream, you can rely upon good fortune, varying according to the accuracy of your aim. If you miss, then you may expect difficulties, owing to some careless. or ill-advised action of your own.

BOX.—This dream also depends upon the circumstances. If you open a Box and find something inside, it is fortunate, but if the Box is empty, then your plans will be upset.

BOXING MATCH.—An astonishing announcement will be made in your hearing leading to important events for you. Be wary of repeating or of writing about it.

BRACELET.—This is either a sign of money or of some love affair. If your affections are concerned, it is a fortunate sign to possess, to wear, or to find a Bracelet, especially if it is of gold. Otherwise you will be lucky in some unexpected financial matter. If you lose, or drop your Bracelet, then you may expect a monetary loss or a broken love affair.

BRAMBLES.—These represent difficulties, and indicate poverty or privation. If you push through, without serious harm from the thorns, then you will overcome your troubles.

BRANCH.—Trees are fortunate, being one of Nature's own blessings. See also **HEDGES.**

BRANCHES.—If in your dream you see a Tree with many fertile Branches, it is a most fortunate omen. But be careful if you see any dead or broken Branches. See also **TREES.**

BRANDY.—Some good news is on the way.

BRAVERY.—This warns the dreamer to keep a cool head and act with all courage, as an emergency is at hand which will test his nerve.

BRASS.—Observe your associates closely and do not let a false friend make you unhappy.

BRAY.—You may expect to hear about the loss of an old friend if you hear a donkey Braying in your dream.

BREAD.—If the Bread is new and pleasant to the taste, it is a sign of physical well-being, bodily comfort. But if it is stale and hard, then domestic worries of a commonplace character are indicated. To bake Bread is an unfortunate omen.

BREAK.—To damage anything in a dream is a very bad sign, generally concerning the health.

BREAKFAST.—An omen of misfortune in a dream; be careful or your own ill-considered actions will plunge you in trouble.

BREAST.—If you dream that you are resting on the Breast of some person, it is a sign of true and loyal friendship.

BREATH.—To dream that you are out of Breath, or exhausted, is a warning of coming trouble.

BREEZE.—To dream you are in a strong wind presages a successful speculation.

BRIARS AND BRAMBLES.—If they prick you, secret enemies will do you an injury; if they draw blood, expect heavy losses in trade. If you dream you pass through them without harm, you will triumph over enemies and become happy.

BRIBE.—A dream of contrary. If you accept a money

Bribe in your dream, it is a sign of upright and honourable conduct on your part.

BRIDE, BRIDEGROOM, OR BRIDESMAIDS.—Unfortunately, this is a dream of contrary. If you are one of these parties, it foretells some great disappointment.

BRIDGE.—To dream that you are crossing a Bridge foretells a change of situation or occupation in business, or a change of district. This will be fortunate if you cross the Bridge without much trouble or delay. If the Bridge is damaged, or being repaired, then be careful and do not make any fresh plans without due thought.

BRISTLES.—These mean social successes and " fine feathers."

BRONCHITIS.—Most dream illnesses are fortunate signs, though they should be treated as signs of obstacles. If you go on well, and recover your health, it is a sign of great prosperity in the near future.

BROOCH.—To dream that you are wearing jewellery depends upon the surroundings for its importance. If you are at home, it is a fortunate omen, but if you wear it at a strange house, then expect trouble.

BROOK OR RUNNING WATER.—Faithful friends, if the stream is clear. Otherwise, be careful.

BROOM.—Beware of a false friend.

BROTH.—To dream that you are taking Broth is a fortunate sign. Your affairs will prosper.

BROTHER.—This omen depends upon the sex of the dreamer. If a woman dreams of her Brother, it is a sign of much domestic happiness ; but if it is a man, then expect a quarrel.

BROWN.—Beware of treachery on the part of someone whom you trust.

BRUISES.—A warning to all but the most robust that their health is suffering from overstrain.

BRUSH.—Should you touch or use a Brush in your dream your greatest wish will shortly be granted.

BUBBLES.—A sign of gaiety. Avoid dissipation, or you may lose your sweetheart.

BUCKLE.—For a woman to dream that the Buckle of her belt has come unfastened foretells trouble and difficulty. All mishaps with one's clothes are bad signs.

BUGLE CALL.—This announces success to your efforts.

BUGS.—A warning to act cautiously as there are unfortunate influences around you.

BUILDING.—To dream of Buildings indicates some change in life, and your success, or otherwise, will depend upon the general appearance—if the Buildings are small, you will not prove successful.

BULL.—The sign of some enemy or rival in love or business.

BULL-DOG.—Good news from an absent friend.

BULL'S-EYE.—To hit the centre of the target is a lucky dream, whereas it is unfortunate to miss it. If you see someone else shooting, be careful about giving your confidence.

BUNION.—Presages the return of a traveller from a great distance.

BURDEN.—To carry some Burden in a dream, shows that you will be dependent upon other people.

BURGLAR.—Beware of treachery among those you trust.

BURIAL.—A dream of contrary, for it denotes a Wedding, though this may not be your own. See also **FUNERAL.**

BURNING HOUSES.—A sign of improved fortunes.

BURNS.—If you Burn yourself in a dream, it is a sign of valuable friendship in your life.

BUSHES.—A change is indicated ; if you push through them the change will be for the better.

BUSINESS DOCUMENT.—To dream of such Papers is a bad sign for a business man, but not for a woman. Be careful of your speculations and investments.

BUTCHER.—You will meet with someone you have not seen for a long time. Act cautiously as this is not a lucky dream.

BUTTER.—This is a good dream, but of a material character, such as feasting. It is usually something of a surprise. See also **MILK.** If you are making Butter, some money will reach you unexpectedly.

BUTTERFLY.—A sign of happiness if you see a gaily coloured Butterfly in the sunshine ; but if it is a Moth, and seen indoors, then it means some slight trouble.

BUTTERMILK.—To drink it indicates disappointment in love. To the married, trouble, sorrow and losses.

BUTTONS.—For a man, this omen shows delay or difficulty in love affairs, but it is fortunate for a woman.

BUY.—To dream that you are Buying a lot of articles is a warning of coming troubles ; be careful with your money matters. But if, in your dream, you are carefully considering every shilling you spend, then it is a fortunate sign.

C

CAB.—To dream that you are riding in a Cab or Taxi shows good fortune, probably in connection with some distant country, or through some friend who is living abroad.

CABBAGES.—A sign of health and long life.

CABIN.—To dream that you are in the Cabin of a ship foretells domestic troubles.

CABINET or WARDROBE.—Beware of treachery among those you trust.

CACKLE.—A sign whose meaning varies very much in different localities. It is best to treat it as a warning that care is needed.

CADDY.—You will receive a present which should have arrived sooner.

CAGE.—To dream that you see birds in a Cage is a token of a successful love affair. But if the Cage is empty, the engagement will probably be broken off.

CAIN.—An unusual dream, distinctly warning the

dreamer to retrace his footsteps and tread a different path.

CAKE.—Food generally denotes good health, provided it is of an enjoyable kind.

CALENDAR.—To dream that you are worrying about some date, is a sign of a fortunate marriage, unless you fail to find out what you seek.

CALF.—A good omen for lovers and married people.

CALICO.—Extremes of experience will be your lot; both happy and unhappy events will colour your life within the next twelve months.

CALLS.—To hear your own name called aloud in your dream is fortunate for those in love. It has no money meaning.

CAMEL.—As with all unusual animals, this foretells difficulties and worries.

CAMERA.—To look into one, someone will deceive you.

CAMPHOR.—Evil speaking will surround you. Do not allow it to vex you.

CAMP.—To dream of soldiers in Camp is also fortunate for love affairs, for it is a dream of contrary, and indicates peace in your domestic affairs.

CAN.—Good news. To drink out of a Can, great joy.

CANAL.—This dream follows the rules for all water conditions. If the water is clean and clear, it is a fortunate sign, but if the water is muddy, or covered with weed, then it is an omen of coming trouble.

CANARY.—A certain sign of a cheerful and comfortable home.

CANDLE.—This is a good omen, provided the Candle burns brightly. But if it is extinguished, you may expect trouble.

CANDY.—Peace and happiness in your home affairs.

CANE.—To dream that you have been whipped is a very bad omen—beware of all business transactions for at least a couple of days.

CANOE.—A Canoe is only intended for one person, and such a dream omen indicates a lack of friends.

CANNIBALS.—Disturbing information will vex and hamper you, but you have little to fear.

CANNISTER.—Should you enclose anything in the Cannister, you will soon have a secret to keep. Should you open one, you will discover a friend's secret.

CANNON.—To dream that you hear the firing of guns or muskets is a certain sign of some vexatious disappointment.

CAP.—If you put on your Cap or Hat, in your dream, it signifies difficulty in your love affairs. If a Cap or Hat is given to you, then you will marry happily.

CAPTAIN.—Advancement, prosperity and hopes fulfilled after great difficulties have been overcome.

CAPTIVITY.—If, in your dream, you see yourself a Captive or in prison, it is a sign of an unhappy marriage.

CARDS.—Playing at Cards in a dream, or watching other people at play, is an indication of coming quarrels.

CARESS.—For a mother to dream that she is Caressing her children is a dream of contrary—she will have anxious days on account of illness.

CAROLS.—To sing them presages a happy marriage.

CARPENTER.—To see workmen busily engaged is a sign that you will overcome your difficulties.

CARPET.—To dream that you are in a room containing a handsome Carpet is a fortunate dream.

CARRIAGE or CART.—To dream that you are driving in a Cart, is a sign of loss of money and position.

CARRY.—To be Carried by anyone in your dream is an uncertain omen—if you are Carried by a woman or by a poor person, it is a fortunate sign, not otherwise.

CARRION or CARCASE OF AN ANIMAL.—Happiness and long life.

CARROTS.—This dream signifies profit by inheritance.

CARVING.—This omen depends upon the circumstances. If you are serving yourself, it shows your own prosperity, but if you are Carving for other people, then someone else will benefit by your actions.

CASCADE.—Happiness and success of a mediocre quality, nothing brilliant but at least freedom from want.

CASHIER.—To imagine yourself in charge of other people's money is a bad omen ; expect financial worry or even loss.

CASTLE.—This omen has varying meanings, but is generally held to indicate a quarrel through your own bad temper. In some places, it is said to show a marriage that opens well, but drifts into difficulties.

CASTOR OIL.—Medicines in a dream are omens of contrary. The more unpleasant the dose, the better it will be for the dreamer.

CAT.—An unfavourable dream, as is the case if you dream of a Dog. It is a dream of contrary and shows unexpected deceit by some one whom you trust.

CATARACT.—This is really a dream of water, so the meaning will depend upon the state of the stream. If the water is clear and running easily, then expect domestic happiness.

CATECHISM.—Your work will shortly be amongst figures and reckoning. Be accurate in small details and good may follow.

CATERPILLARS.—An unfortunate omen—trouble from a secret rival or enemy.

CATHEDRAL.—The important nature of this building has led to many contrary definitions. It seems best to treat the outside view of a Cathedral as showing good fortune, while if you dream of the interior, you should take care, or trouble may befall you.

CATTLE.—A sign of prosperity in business, but if you see yourself driving Cattle, it shows that you have to work hard. Black Cattle, however, show trouble in business, owing to the unfortunate colour.

CAULIFLOWER.—Like most vegetables, this is an omen of good health and a comfortable home life.

CAVALRY.—To dream that you see mounted troops is a sign of good fortune in your love affairs.

CAVE.—An obstacle dream. If you escape from the Cave, all will go well, though you must expect trouble at first. But if you fall into a Cave, or fail to get out, then expect business worries.

CAUSEWAY.—Your troubles will increase and then cease abruptly, especially if you should dream you cross over one and if your work is of an artistic nature.

CEILING.—If in your dream, anything happens to the room in which you find yourself, it is an omen of trouble through a friend, probably due to severe illness.

CELERY.—Another useful vegetable—such a dream means good health and domestic comfort.

CELLAR.—An obstacle dream, unless there is plenty of coal in the Cellar, when it indicates good business from a distance, perhaps abroad.

CEMENT.—A present is soon to be given you, which will lead to more important events.

CERTIFICATE.—You do not attempt to see things from other people's point of view. Try to be more sympathetic in small ways and big events will ensue.

CEMETERY.—You will conquer all things.

CHAFF.—Your plans will not succeed.

CHAINS.—A dream of contrary, showing that you will escape from some difficulty that worries you at the moment. But a gold Chain round a woman's neck shows good fortune from some friend or lover.

CHAIR.—To see an empty Chair in your dream indicates news from a long-absent friend.

CHALK.—To dream of Chalk cliffs means disappointment in some cherished hope.

CHAMPAGNE.—This is an unfortunate omen for love affairs.

CHAMPIONS.—To dream that you are successful in sports or games is a sign of poor success in business affairs. Pull yourself together and be more careful.

CHAPEL.—As with all religious buildings, it is a fortunate dream if you see the outside, but not if you find yourself inside.

CHARITY.—This is a dream of contrary—the more charitable you are in your dream, the less fortune awaits you in your business affairs.

CHASTISE.—This is a dream of contrary—if you find yourself thrashing your children in your dream, it indicates a happy and prosperous home life. But if you yourself are being thrashed, then it shows bad fortune in money matters.

CHATTER.—A runaway marriage will cause much gossip.

CHEATING.—To dream that you have been Cheated, is a fortunate omen; but take care if you yourself Cheat someone else in your dream.

CHEEKS.—It is a good omen to dream of your Cheeks or face, especially for a woman.

CHEERING.—The sound of shouting or Cheering in your dreams is an unfortunate omen. Be careful of your actions.

CHEESE.—Annoyance and deception from those around you. To eat Cheese shows worry through your own hasty action.

CHEMIST.—A Chemist's shop is not a good subject for a dream; be warned as to your business dealings.

CHEQUE.—It is always a bad sign, in a dream, when you receive paper instead of cash. Be careful or you will sustain a loss.

CHERRIES.—To see Cherries growing is an omen of coming misfortune; you will be wise to move slowly in your business affairs.

CHESS and DRAUGHTS.—To dream that you are playing one of these games shows difficulties in your path. The issue will depend upon the result of the game.

CHEST.—To dream of a large Box concerns your love affairs; if the Chest is empty, prepare for a disappointment.

CHESTNUTS.—Domestic affliction.

CHEW.—If you dream you are Chewing, you have to

overlook another's fault before you will know peace of mind and happiness.

CHICKENS.—All very young animals show friendships.

CHILBLAINS.—A misunderstanding will be cleared up.

CHILDREN.—A lucky dream, showing success in business.

CHIMNEY.—To see a tall chimney predicts fortunate events.

CHINA.—Financial gains from a long distance.

CHIPS.—A business success or wager won.

CHISEL.—A public appearance of some kind.

CHOCOLATES or SWEETS.—To be eating Sweets in a dream is a sign of a coming gift.

CHOIR.—As the Choir is part of the interior of a sacred building, it is not really a fortunate sign. If the Choirboys are singing, you will hear from an old friend.

CHOKING.—Strangely enough, it is a fortunate sign to find yourself Choking in your dream.

CHRISTENING.—This dream also has to do with the interior of a sacred building ; it is not a fortunate omen.

CHRISTMAS.—A good omen, but it refers more particularly to your friends or your family affairs, and not to business.

CHURCH.—Here again, it is the outside of the building that is fortunate. To dream that you are inside a sacred building is a warning of coming trouble.

CHURCHYARD.—Although apparently unpleasant, this is a fortunate dream as it concerns the outside of a church.

CHURNING.—To dream that you are Churning is a sign of prosperity and plenty. To the single, happy marriage.

CIDER.—Gossip about your own private affairs. Act cautiously.

CIGAR.—It is a fortunate dream to see yourself smoking. Prosperity awaits you.

CIGARETTE.—To dream you are lighting one signifies new plans ; a half-smoked Cigarette held in the hand is a postponement, to smoke it to the end, means a successful conclusion to your hopes.

CINDERS.—Ashes or Cinders in a dream is a bad sign—expect disappointment.

CIRCUS.—A sign of future unhappiness, due to your own careless habits.

CISTERN.—Should you see it brimful, it is a good sign of financial matters improving.

CITY.—A large City denotes ambition, if in the distance, successfully attained should you enter it in your dream.

CLARET.—To dream that you are drinking red wine is not a good sign ; be careful in your business dealings.

CLERGYMAN.—This is a dream of disappointment. Strictly speaking, it concerns the inside of a church, which is never a fortunate omen.

CLIMBING.—It is a sign of business prosperity to find yourself Climbing, unless the effort proves too great for your strength. Still, even then it shows some sort of good fortune, though combined with difficulties.

CLIFFS.—A dangerous dream. Do not take any risks, especially of high places from which you might slip, for some time.

CLOCK.—To dream that you hear a Clock strike the hours is a fortunate sign. You will enjoy a comfortable life.

CLOGS.—To dream you put them on, prepare for a wedding shortly.

CLOTHES.—This is a dream of contrary—if you have plenty of clothes in your dream, it is a warning of coming trouble ; if you are partly dressed, or naked, then prosperity is coming your way. To put on Clothes is a fortunate sign, but if you make any error, you must not correct it, or you will spoil your luck.

CLOUDS.—This dream depends upon the circumstances ; if the sky is stormy and dark, it betokens many sorrows. But if the Clouds pass away, then better fortune awaits you.

CLOVER.—To dream that you are in a Clover field is

a very fortunate sign, especially to those who are in love.

CLOWN.—Others think you witless.

CLUB.—You will meet with people whom you have not seen for a long time. Do not let them influence you.

COACH.—It is not a very good omen when you dream that you are driving in a Coach ; be careful, or you may find yourself in difficulties.

COAL.—This is a warning of danger. If you dream that you are in a Coal-pit, it is serious, and means heavy business losses, or a keen disappointment in love. To see Coal burning brightly in a grate is, however, a fortunate sign, as the sinister black colour has been destroyed.

COAT.—This is a sign of contrary—if you are wearing a new Coat, beware of business troubles. If your Coat is old, or if you tear it in any way, then prosperity is coming to you.

COAT-OF-ARMS.—To dream of a shield with a Coat-of-arms on it is an excellent sign. A powerful friend will protect you.

COAXING.—A dream signifying a dangerous request probably to be made to you. Do not accede to it.

COBBLER.—Misfortune, which you will overcome, with good fortune to follow.

COBWEB.—To brush one away means a triumph for you over an enemy.

COCKCHAFER.—Business troubles.

COCKLES.—Expect bad news from afar.

COCK.—Although a Cock is a bad omen by itself, it is considered a sign of some unexpected good news if you hear the bird crowing.

COCOA.—This is a good omen, but only concerns your domestic life, not your business affairs.

COFFEE.—This dream also is favourable, and signifies great domestic happiness.

COFFIN.—Emblematic of the serious illness of some dear friend, perhaps even death, if there is much Black seen.

COGWHEELS.—Introductions will cause a fresh outlook on your affairs. Take new hope and achieve your plans fearlessly from now onward.

COINS.—To dream of money in the shape of Coins, is on the whole favourable. But the more important the coin, the less fortunate the dream. Copper coins are more favourable than silver, while gold is often considered a bad omen, as is the case with paper money.

COLD.—If you feel Cold, it is a sign of comfort and friendship.

COLLAR.—It is a good sign for a lover to dream that he is putting on a new Collar, whereas a soiled Collar shows fickleness on the part of the loved one.

COLLEGE.—It is not a fortunate omen for a man or woman to dream that they are at College.

COLLIERY.—Owing to the prevalence of black, a Colliery is not a very auspicious omen ; there will be a certain amount of contentment, but not full satisfaction.

COLONEL or OFFICER.—A sign of contrary if a woman dreams that she has married an Officer or other official of rank. The higher the importance of the dream person, the less satisfactory will be the realisation.

COLOURS.—If you dream about Flags or Decorations in many bright colours, it signifies continued prosperity and success in all your undertakings. **WHITE** is always favourable, especially in matters concerning other people, such as public affairs. **BLACK** is the sinister colour, unless you dream of a funeral, in which case it is appropriate, and signifies only a struggle before success. **BLUE** and **PURPLE** represent prosperity through other people, good fortune in your love affairs, and so on. **SCARLET** or **RED** is a warning of quarrels, the loss of friends ; but **CRIMSON** denotes pleasant news from an unexpected quarter. **YELLOW** and **ORANGE** are mental tints, and show that you need not expect any important change in your affairs for some time. **GREEN** indicates a journey, or business with people at a distance.

COLLECTION.—Should you dream you are contributing to a Collection, you have to travel a long way soon, but will meet with good luck abroad.

COLLISION.—A sign of mental strife. You will need all your self-control to overcome the effect of bad tidings.

COLUMBINE.—The flower is a sign of a visit to luxurious surroundings.

COLUMN.—This presages future success and honours.

COMBAT.—It is not a good sign to be engaged in a fight in a dream; if you are successful, all will come well, but only after difficulty and worry.

COMBING.—To dream that you are Combing your hair, or that of some other person, is a sign of loss through someone you trust.

COMET or STAR.—The usual heavenly bodies, such as **SUN, MOON or STARS,** are fortunate signs and indicate success in your affairs. But a **COMET** is out of the ordinary, and all such unusual signs are warnings of coming trouble.

COMFORT.—It is an omen of contrary to dream that you are living in Comfort and luxury.

COMMAND.—To dream you Command anyone, signifies trouble; to dream you see one Commanding, signifies anger and authority.

COMPANION.—To dream that you are with a pleasant Companion is a fortunate omen; it shows immediate success.

COMPETING IN SPORTS.—This is a bad sign, and the more successful the competition, the worse for the dreamer.

COMPLEXION.—To dream you see an unknown person of a brown Complexion, is a sign of glory and success. If one dreams he sees a woman of a very brown Complexion, it signifies a very dangerous illness.

CONCERT.—To find yourself at a Concert in your dream is a sign of unexpected news.

CONFECTIONS.—To dream that one makes Confections and Sweetmeats betokens pleasure and profit.

CONFESSION.—Guard the confidences given to you by others, as you will shortly be strongly tempted to reveal a secret.

CONFETTI.—Social disappointments of a trifling nature.

CONFUSION.—To dream of a disturbance or Confusion presages loneliness and trouble. Keep to frequented paths.

CONGREGATION.—As with all omens concerning the interior of a chur h, this is not a fortunate sign.

CONGRATULATIONS.—These signify cause for condolence, but better times to follow.

CONJUROR.—To dream of seeing Conjuring tricks, a mystery will be solved.

CONSCIENCE.—It is a dream of contrary if you are being worried by your Conscience—all will go well. The more self-satisfied you feel, the less your chance of prosperity.

CONVICTED.—To be found guilty in a Court of Justice is a good sign ; prosperity is on the way.

CONSENT.—If you dream that you Consent to the request of someone, it denotes a discovery of lost valuables.

CONTENT.—Another " contrary " dream. Be careful of fires and enemies alike for a time. There is danger for you in both.

CONTRADICTION.—Your wish will be granted.

CONVENT.—An engagement speedily followed by a happy though not wealthy wedding.

CONVULSIONS.—To dream you see someone in Convulsions means an invitation to a concert.

COOKING.—To dream of Cooking, whether by yourself or someone else, is a good sign, but only concerns material comforts.

COPPERS.—These are luckiest when you dream of bestowing them on someone else ; given to you they signify loss.

COPYING.—This foretells legal affairs, probably to your advantage.

CORAL.—To dream you are wearing it predicts the return of an old friend or a meeting with a former sweetheart.

CORD.—To knot a Cord means the strengthening of a friendship ; to unravel it means the breaking of an engagement.

CORKS.—If you dream that you are extracting a Cork, it is a sign of some good news of a friend. If you are pushing a Cork into a bottle, it shows a visit to you unexpectedly.

CORKSCREW.—It is a sign of illness to use a Corkscrew in your dream.

CORN or CORNFIELD.—A very fortunate dream, and a sign of money in plenty, according to the state of the growing Corn.

CORNERS.—In a mild degree, a Corner is an obstacle dream. It is not a good sign unless you leave the Corner for the open.

CORNET.—Family quarrels are foretold when you hear a Cornet being played.

CORNS.—To dream that you have Corns on your feet, is a sign of fortunate business ventures.

CORPSE.—An omen of estrangement or separation from friends, through your own fault ; an unhappy love affair.

COTTAGE.—It is a fortunate sign to find yourself living in a Cottage, unless you are discontented and endeavour to get away.

COUGHING.—This is a dream of contrary, and indicates good health, vigour, and business prosperity.

COUNTERFEIT.—If you handle Counterfeit coins in a dream, you will be asked to help someone who will make you a good friend.

COUNTERPANE.—The sign of an accident, if it is torn or pulled from the bed.

COURT.—To dream of going to Court means a business loss.

COURT-PLASTER.—To be binding a cut with Court-plaster means a recovery from a long-standing illness.

COURTSHIP.—This also is a dream of contrary, for the more fortunate your wooing in your dreams, the worse it will be for your real love affairs.

COUSIN.—To dream of your relatives is a sign that you may soon receive unexpected news.

COW or BULL.—Good luck, unless you are pursued by the animal, in which case it depends upon what happens. If you escape the Cow, you will survive the evil schemes of some enemy. The greater the number of animals seen, the more serious the warning.

COWSLIPS.—If you see wildflowers in your dream, it is generally a good sign, though the good fortune may come from some unexpected source.

CRAB.—As in the case of all unusual creatures, this is a sign of coming difficulties.

CRADLE.—It is not a good sign to dream of an empty Cradle; misfortune will come, probably through ill-health.

CRANE.—You are believing something to be lost which is not far away from you.

CRAWL.—An omen of difficulty; your love affairs will not prosper.

CREW.—It is not a good omen if you see Sailors at work on a vessel; expect bad news.

CRIBBAGE.—To dream of taking part in a game signifies important decisions for you to make. To watch the game, your advice will be asked. Think well before giving it.

CRIES.—These are omens of contrary—if the Cries are happy and joyous, then expect bad news. But if they are cries of trouble or distress, then all will go well.

CRIMSON.—See COLOURS.

CRIMES.—Your undertakings will be crowned with success.

CRIPPLE.—A warning to be kind to those around you

CROCHET.—A change in your environment leading to better times.

CROCODILE.—Another warning of troubles ahead.

CROCUS.—All early flowers are fortunate omens in a dream.

CROSS.—An omen of sorrow in the affections.

CROSS-PURPOSES.—To dream you are at Cross-purposes with someone signifies joy, pleasure, health and concord among friends and relations, and prosperity.

CROSS-ROADS.—To the unmarried, an engagement will soon be made, either by you or amongst your friends.

CROW.—The sinister colour, **BLACK,** makes this bird an omen of grief, and misfortune. If more than one Crow is seen, the matter becomes very serious.

CROWDS.—Your happiness is assured and will increase.

CROWN.—To dream that you have a Crown on your head is a sign that you will benefit through people in a better position than yourself. If a Cross is seen as well, then you will benefit through a death.

CRUCIFIX.—This omen is associated with the interior of a church, so it is not a favourable sign.

CRUST.—To be reduced to eating Crusts is a good dream ; your business affairs will be prosperous.

CRUELTY.—To dream of seeing this means that one near to you is in need of help.

CRUMBS.—To dream of birds pecking at Crumbs foretells both gifts and good tidings.

CRUTCHES.—This is an obstacle dream—if you recover and are able to walk without the aid of the Crutches, all will go well. If not, expect trouble.

CRYSTAL.—You will soon be shown the " turning " in the " long lane " that has been worrying you.

CUBS.—A friendly hint will be given you which if taken will avert danger.

CUCKOO.—A dream signifying misfortune in love affairs, or in the marriage state.

CUCUMBER.—A sign of good health, or more often, recovery from an illness.

CUP.—An empty Cup is a bad omen, but a full one is a sign of prosperity.

CUPBOARD.—To dream of an empty Cupboard is a bad sign for your business prosperity. If you put things inside, it shows that you will recover your losses after some distress.

CURATE.—To dream of a Curate is a sign of trouble over your love affairs. Avoid quarrels.

CURRANTS.—This dream depends upon the Colour of the fruit ; these gifts of Nature are always fortunate, but in this case the colour, Black, is an exception.

CURLS.—A complete change in your affairs ; new environment and better times in view.

CURSE.—To dream of hearing Curses and rough language presages a visit of ceremony.

CURTAIN.—This is an obstacle dream, but refers particularly to bad faith in someone you trust. If you pull the Curtain aside, you will be warned in time.

CUSHION.—Signs of Comfort in your dreams are not fortunate. The more comfortable you find yourself, the greater will be your difficulties and business worries.

CUTTLEFISH.—Important decisions to be made in a great hurry.

CYCLING.—To dream that you are Cycling foretells a visit that you will make at some distance. To see people Cycling, friends from afar will visit you.

CYPRESS.—An unfortunate dream, usually a premonition of trouble. Be cautious and it may be avoided.

D

DAFFODILS.—All early Spring flowers are fortunate omens. Daffodils particularly concern your love affairs, not your business concerns. A happy future is certain for the one who dreams of these beautiful Spring flowers ; but for the best results they should be seen out-of-doors.

DAGGERS or KNIVES.—Be careful of treachery, or you will suffer heavy loss.

DAHLIA.—Financial affairs will improve shortly.

DAMSON.—To see them, anxiety ; to eat them, trouble through false companions.

DAIRY.—A fortunate dream. See **BUTTER.**

DAISIES.—These simple wildflowers are always fortunate omens in your dreams.

DANCE or DANCING.—If you dream that you are Dancing, it is a sign that money is coming to you, or that some cherished plan will meet with success. But if you merely watch others Dancing, then you will hear of good fortune concerning a friend.

DANDELIONS.—These common yellow flowers are fortunate for love affairs or married life.

DANGER.—This is an omen of contrary. If you face Danger in your dreams, you may expect success ; but if you avoid it, then trouble will come.

DARKNESS.—To dream that you are in the Dark is a sign of difficulties ahead ; if you fall or hurt yourself, then you may expect a change for the worse, but if you succeed in groping your way to the light, then you will face your troubles successfully.

DAUGHTER.—To dream of your Children is generally considered a contrary vision. What affects your girls in your dream will concern your boys in real life.

DARNING.—To dream you are Darning denotes the introduction of a new and kindly friend. To see it is a warning against gossip.

DATES.—You are likely to be admired by some member of the other sex.

DAWN.—To see the Dawn, days of storm and stress lie ahead.

DEAD or DEATH.—This omen depends upon the circumstances, but on the whole, it concerns other people, not the dreamer. If you speak to friends or relatives who are Dead, it means news of some living friend or relation; if you touch or kiss them, the news will be of a sorrowful nature. To dream of a Death means news of a birth.

DEAD MARCH.—To dream of hearing this played portends good luck to one whom you care for.

DEATH-WATCH BEETLE.—To dream of this ill-omened insect presages a speedy marriage.

DEATH'S HEAD.—You may discover some hidden secret.

DEAFNESS.—To find yourself suddenly Deaf in your dream is a good sign. By some unexpected turn of events you will escape a great trouble or difficulty.

DEBTS.—To pay your Debts in a dream is a good omen, but if other people repay what they owe you, then expect a loss.

DECORATE.—To dream that you are beautifying your room or your house is a dream of contrary. Expect losses in your business affairs.

DEEDS.—Should you dream of signing them, avoid speculation and quarrels with those dear to you, as you are in danger of loss either of money or affection.

DEER.—To dream of wild animals in unnatural captivity is unfavourable, and indicates quarrels or disputes.

DEFEND.—To dream of shielding or Defending someone denotes at least one loyal friend.

DEFORMITY.—To dream that you are Deformed signifies shame and sorrow.

DELIRIUM.—To dream of being Delirious signifies danger through a secret; to see someone else in that condition means a friend trying to help you secretly.

DELICATE.—To dream of ill-health is always a good sign. You will be vigorous and go ahead in your business.

DELIGHT.—Excessive happiness in your dreams is a bad omen. Expect trouble at home and business worries.

DELUGE.—A heavy downpour of rain is an omen of bad luck in your love affairs. Avoid quarrels.

DENTIST.—A dream of illness.

DERBY.—A lucky dream; financial gain will come your way.

DESERT.—To dream that you are travelling across a Desert, or a wide open space, signifies difficulties concerning some cherished plan. It is particularly bad if you encounter bad weather or other troubles. If the sun is shining, then the final outcome will be successful.

DESK.—This dream depends upon whether the Desk is locked or open. If locked, then you may expect bad news; but if you are sitting at an open Desk, then all will go well.

DESPAIR.—To dream that you are seriously troubled is an omen of contrary. It shows domestic happiness.

DESSERT.—It is always a very fortunate omen to dream that you are eating ripe fruit. If the fruit, however, is not ripe, or has been kept too long, expect business losses.

DESTROY.—It is a most unfortunate omen if you break or destroy something of value in your dream.

DETECTIVE.—You will hear a confession that will rectify an important mistake in your opinion of someone.

DETEST or DISLIKE.—To dream that you Dislike anyone is a bad sign—it shows a coming quarrel with an old friend or a close relative.

DEVIL.—It is a very bad dream if you imagine you see Satan, but the outcome will depend upon the circumstances. Whatever happens, however, it means a long struggle.

DEVOTION.—As with most dreams concerning Religion, this is a good sign. See **ABBEY, CHURCH, CLERGY-MEN,** and similar words.

DEW.—One of Nature's blessings. A very fortunate omen in a dream if you see Dew on the grass.

DIAMONDS.—There is no certainty about this dream,

as some authorities call it an omen of misfortune, while others declare that it shows some fortunate deal in business or speculation. Probably it depends upon the financial and social position of the dreamer, and should be considered a dream of contrary.

DICE.—To dream that you are playing with Dice is a sure sign of changing fortunes, but it depends upon circumstances which way things will go.

DICTIONARY.—This denotes quarrels and the loss of a friend.

DIFFICULTY.—A dream of obstacles. If you succeed in overcoming your difficulty, all will be well.

DIGGING.—This dream depends upon the nature of the soil, for it is emblematic. If the soil is good and easily worked, your plans will succeed. It concerns money, not personal affairs.

DINNER.—All meals are dreams of contrary—the better the Dinner, the greater the difficulties ahead of you.

DIRT.—To dream that your clothes are Dirty denotes sorrow; if you yourself are personally unclean or unwashed, it means illness.

DIPLOMA.—You have neglected a talent, which, properly trained, might lead you to success.

DISASTERS.—These are always dreams of contrary— it is a favourable dream for business people.

DISAPPOINTMENT.—To dream you are Disappointed assures the reader of success in the very matter dreamed about.

DISCUSSION.—It is a good omen if you have a friendly Discussion in your dream; but not if you lose your temper.

DISEASE.—To dream that you are ill is a warning of treachery; it is very unfavourable in the case of lovers. See **ACHE, ILLNESS.**

DISFIGUREMENT.—To dream of personal Disfigurement presages an unexpected happiness.

DISGRACE.—A dream of contrary—it is a fortunate sign if you find yourself in trouble or disgrace.

DISGUISE.—Fancy costume is not a fortunate sign; it shows trouble, but not of a serious nature.

DISH.—To break a plate or Dish is a bad sign—it shows domestic trouble.

DISHONESTY.—An important document will be mislaid. If you are Dishonest in your dream, it will be a document affecting your affairs.

DISLIKE.—This dream depends upon the circumstances. If you dream that someone does not like you, and that you are worried, it is a bad omen. If, however, you do not appear to be upset at all, then your difficulties will be overcome.

DISMISS.—To dream of being Dismissed from a business position presages a rise in position.

DISPUTES.—A dream of contrary, it signifies success, but there will be obstacles in the way at first.

DISOBEDIENCE.—To dream of your own Disobedience denotes a difficult choice before you, possibly regarding marriage.

DISTANCE.—A dream that you are separated from your friends or family is a bad sign; but if you dream of some person who is separated from you, then you will hear good news.

DISTRESS.—Another omen of contrary. It is a good sign if you dream that you are in Distress, or in trouble of any sort.

DISTRUST.—To dream that you doubt some person is a bad omen; it is just as serious if someone else Distrusts you.

DITCH.—All obstacles of a material kind are bad signs—beware of unexpected difficulties, especially in money matters.

DIVING.—To dream that you are Diving, or falling into water, is a sign of loss of money in speculation, or in some risky business undertaking.

DIVORCE.—It is a dream of contrary—if you imagine you are being Divorced it is a sign of domestic happiness.

DRENCHED.—An unfortunate dream, presaging danger of fever for you or someone near to you.

DRESS.—It is always a good sign if you are concerned about your clothes in a dream. You will succeed in your plans.

DRINK.—If you dream that you are thirsty and cannot find water, it shows misfortune. If the water is dirty or muddy, it is a bad sign, as also if it is warm or hot. But to Drink clear fresh water is a very good sign. It is also fortunate to Drink milk. See **MILK, WINE.**

DRIVING.—It is a fortunate dream if someone else is Driving you; but if you yourself are the Driver, then expect money losses.

DROPS.—If you are measuring out the Drops, you will shortly have a small sum of money left you.

DROPSY.—Bodily sickness.

DROUGHT.—To dream of very dry weather and parched fields is a bad omen. Beware of business losses.

DROWN.—A most unfortunate dream for business people. But if someone rescues you, then you may expect help from a friend.

DRUGS.—A successful speculation; much gossip around you.

DRUMS.—It is a fortunate omen to hear Drums in your dreams. You will gain great success.

DRUNK.—To dream that you are intoxicated, is a warning of financial troubles. If you see someone else who is Drunk, then you will lose money through some other person.

DUCKS or GEESE.—A good sign. If the Geese attack you, it means trouble in business affairs.

DUET.—To sing in a Duet in your dreams is a good sign for the lover, or for the married. It shows much domestic happiness.

DUEL.—Trouble from friends and relatives. You have treacherous enemies.

DYING.—If you dream you are dying, you will receive empty promises.

DIZZINESS.—An unhoped-for success, probably an engagement.

DOCTOR.—A good dream financially.

DOGS.—This dream depends upon circumstances. If the Dog is friendly, all will be well ; if he barks, then beware of quarrels, and if he bites you, expect treachery from someone you trust.

DOLLS.—To dream of Dolls is a sign of domestic happiness.

DOMINO.—A small triumph over difficulties.

DONKEY.—See **ASS.**

DOOR.—This is almost an obstacle dream. If you are trying to enter a house, and the Door is not opened, you may expect serious business troubles. If the house or room appears to have many Doors, then beware of speculation, for you will lose your money.

DOVES.—A fortunate dream, but for business and home affairs.

DOWRY.—To receive money in a dream without earning it, is always a bad sign.

DRAGON.—To see one, great riches.

DRAPER.—Small worries ending shortly by the help of a business acquaintance.

DRAWBRIDGE.—You will undertake an unexpected journey.

DRAUGHTS or CHESS.—A somewhat similar dream to Dice. It shows fluctuations of fortune, and you should avoid all speculative business or betting.

DRAWERS.—To dream of an open Drawer is a fortunate omen, but if you cannot open a closed Drawer, then beware of trouble ahead. If a woman dreams of her Drawers or her underclothing, it is a bad sign. She will not be faithful to the man who loves her.

DREAMING.—To dream that you consult anyone about your dreams shows that you may expect news from a distance.

DUMB.—To dream that you cannot speak, or to meet a Dumb person in your dream, is a bad sign. Avoid speculation and do not discuss your business plans.

DUN.—To dream of being Dunned for payment presages financial success.

DUNGEON.—This is an obstacle dream. If you cannot escape from the Dungeon, expect business losses. If you do escape, all will come well, though only after some difficulty.

DUSK.—Darkness is not important in a dream, as it would be in real life, as it is your natural surroundings when asleep. It represents some slight difficulty ahead of you, possibly in your love affairs.

DUST.—Dust or dirt is a bad omen, and shows struggle against adverse circumstances. To dream that you are Dusting a room shows that some improvement will come if you persevere.

DWARF.—If you see a Dwarf in your dream, it is a sign of difficulties in your domestic circle.

DYE.—To dream that you are Dyeing your hair, or rouging your cheeks, is a bad sign. You will suffer through your own folly.

E

EAGLE.—If this noble bird is flying, it signifies good fortune ; if it is dead or wounded, expect loss of money. If, however, the flying bird threatens the dreamer, then you may expect many difficulties.

EAR-RINGS.—This omen in a dream signifies a quarrel. It does not matter whether you wear them, give them to someone, or receive them as a present.

EARS.—To dream of any trouble with your Ears is a bad sign—it shows trouble from some unexpected source.

EARTHQUAKE.—This is a rare dream, and consequently the meaning varies greatly. People in the East think little of such happenings in real life, so in their dream they attach little importance to it—some difficulty to be overcome. But for a Westerner, the omen should be treated far more seriously, and should be looked upon as a warning.

EARWIG.—Beware of enemies; you have one who will cause you trouble.

EASEL.—It is a happy omen to dream that you are an artist, working at an Easel.

EASTER.—To dream of this Church Festival is an omen of coming happiness.

EAST.—You are about to be sent on a long journey with an important result; perhaps a religious mission.

EATING.—An unfortunate omen as a rule, and a sign of family quarrels. But if you see other people Eating in your dream, it shows a valuable friendship. To eat Cheese is fortunate, however. See **FRUIT**, and other similar titles.

EAVESDROPPING.—To dream that you are secretly listening to the conversation of other people is a sign that some unexpected good fortune is coming to you.

EBONY.—A voyage to a foreign country.

ECHO.—This curious dream is a sign that you will hear some good fortune, but not concerning yourself. In some cases, the dreamer may even suffer through the success of some other person.

ECLIPSE.—This omen is sometimes met in dreams, but it is rare. It indicates the illness of someone closely connected with you.

EELS.—When seen in a dream, these indicate difficulties which you can overcome if you persevere.

EGGS.—A sign of money, unless the Eggs are stale, or unpleasant to eat. If the eggshells are broken, it shows loss of money.

ELASTIC.—This dream denotes an improvement in your fortunes.

ELBOW.—Pain in your arm is a warning of difficulty. If it is sufficiently severe to prevent the use of the arm, then be very cautious in your business ventures.

ELDERBERRIES.—An omen of trouble from some friend. But wild fruits are not easily determined when appearing in dreams, so be certain that it is this particular berry.

ELECTION.—To dream that you are assisting at one means a speedy success for your own hopes.

ELECTRICITY.—Something will happen to surprise you greatly. Guard against small losses.

ELEPHANT.—This friendly beast denotes assistance from friends or outside influences.

ELF or FAIRY.—This is a very fortunate dream, for it shows that the " Little People " are friendly.

ELM.—To dream of a lofty tree is a very fortunate omen. Money will come easily all your life.

ELOPEMENT.—A dream of contrary. If you are Eloping with your lover, it shows quarrels and an unhappy marriage. If you see other people Eloping, it is a sign of illness.

EMBRACE.—This is a dream of contrary, for it is not considered fortunate if anyone Embraces you in a dream. But if you see your wife, sweetheart, or friend embracing someone else, then it is a good omen for you.

EMBROIDERY.—See NEEDLEWORK.

EMBANKMENT.—Your hopes will not be fulfilled, but someone you have known formerly will shortly return into your life.

EMERALD.—Various meanings are attached to this beautiful gem. In the East, it is considered the greatest possible good fortune, but in the West it is usually treated as a sign of business with someone at a distance or a separation from some loved one.

EMIGRATION.—A friend in a foreign country will write to you shortly enclosing a present.

EMPLOYMENT.—A dream of contrary. It is a sign of prosperity in business if you dream that you are out of work. To dream that you Employ other people shows that their interests will clash with yours.

EMPTINESS.—To dream you are pouring from an Empty jar signifies unexpected gains, but an Empty barrel means poverty.

END OF THE WORLD.—You will hear of something very surprising leading to good times for yourself.

ENEMY.—To dream that you meet, or are in the company of someone whom you do not like, is an omen of contrary, and foretells good fortune for you.

ENGAGEMENT.—To dream of any Engagement—business, social or matrimonial, is considered a bad sign.

ENGAGEMENT RING.—To see or wear one means a new attraction, or to be Engaged a speedy wedding.

ENGINE.—To dream of machinery in motion is not a good omen. You may expect difficulties in the near future.

ENGRAVE.—To Engrave on metal in a dream means a change of work and residence for the better.

ENLISTMENT.—To dream of Enlisting yourself means a postponed success.

ENJOYMENT.—Usually a dream of contrary, unless there is some obvious reason for your pleasure, such as a wedding. It shows difficulties and disappointments.

ENTERTAINMENT.—This dream depends upon the circumstances. It is usually a very fortunate omen, unless for any reason you feel uncomfortable. If you leave before the Entertainment is over, it is a sign that you will miss some good opportunity through your own carelessness.

ENVELOPES.—Closed Envelopes represent difficulties. If you can open the Envelope and remove the contents, then some worry will be smoothed away.

ENVY.—To dream that other people Envy you is a good sign.

EPAULETS.—For a girl to dream of someone wearing them predicts a military or naval lover ; to a man they portend advancement in business.

EPICURE.—Sickness.

EPITAPH.—A wedding or a new addition to the family should you be already married.

ERMINE.—This signifies a letter from, or some association with those of high rank ; but to the sick, a slow recovery.

ERRAND.—This is really an obstacle dream. If you are out on an Errand, and successfully conclude it, then all will be well. If you cannot procure the article you require, then you may expect business troubles.

ERUPTION.—Good luck is coming to you which will make you much envied.

ESCAPE.—This is a straight dream that depends upon the apparent happenings. If you Escape from any difficulty in your dream, it means success in your personal affairs, a triumph over difficulties. If you Escape from fire or water, you may expect anxious moments, but a successful issue ; if from some wild animal, then look for treachery near you. If in your dream you do not Escape, then it is a very bad sign.

ESTATES.—To dream of your own Estate denotes a devoted marriage partner.

EVENING.—A prosperous time to come later in life. Your earlier worries will be happily ended.

EVE.—To dream that you are Eve, or, in fact, naked, is a fortunate omen for a woman. See **ADAM.**

EVERGREENS or BUSHES AND TREES IN FULL LEAF.—One of the most fortunate of all dreams, for it tells of deep and lasting success, not only in business matters, but also in love affairs.

EVIDENCE.—To dream of giving Evidence against a criminal in court, denotes a friend whose reputation you will be able to save.

EVIL SPIRITS.—A very serious omen, unless you succeed in driving them away. Be careful in your business.

EWE.—A large family and prosperous times to come.

EWER.—Guard your secrets which are in danger, especially should you dream of breaking it.

EXAMINATION.—An obstacle dream. If you find that the Examination is too difficult, then expect business worries. If, however, you can answer most of the questions, and dream that you are doing well, then some unexpected good fortune awaits you.

EXCHANGE.—If you dream that you are Exchanging articles with some other person, expect business losses and difficulties.

EXCISEMAN.—A high official post will be attained either by yourself, or, should the dreamer be a girl, a member of the family.

EXCUSE.—It is a bad sign if you find yourself making Excuses in your dreams. You will suffer loss through your own folly.

EXCITEMENT.—To dream that you are feeling unpleasantly disturbed denotes a successful ending to your plans.

EXCURSION.—Be on your guard against a married associate who may not be a true friend.

EXECUTOR.—Loss of money through another's failure.

EXECUTION.—The success of your undertakings will be doubtful.

EXERCISE.—This might be called an obstacle dream. If you enjoy the vigorous Exercise, all will be well. But if you feel tired, then beware of money losses.

EXHAUSTED.—See **EXERCISE**. In your dream you may not know why you feel Exhausted, but it is always a bad sign unless you recover fully in your dream.

EXHIBITION.—This is really a form of Enjoyment, and is seldom a good omen. Difficulties are ahead, due to your own actions.

EXILE.—To dream that you have been sent away signifies that your lot will be cast largely in foreign parts.

EXPEDITIONS.—See **ERRAND**. This omen is only fortunate if you carry out your purpose. If you set out to go somewhere, or to do something, and fail in your purpose, then expect money losses and worry in business.

EXPLOSION.—Danger to a realtive.

EXPRESS.—If you are travelling in it beware of offending those over you in business.

EXTRAVAGANCE.—An omen of happy domestic surroundings.

EYEBROWS.—To be concerned over your Eyebrows is looked upon as a sign of some unimportant but fortunate event.

EYEGLASS.—Good news from some friend, or sometimes a fortunate business deal.

EYELIDS.—An omen of trouble among those around you. Watch carefully and help if you can.

EYES.—It is considered fortunate to see strange Eyes staring at you in your dream. Some important change will soon take place. But if you are worried about your own Eyes, then be careful in your actions, for someone is working secretly against you.

F

FABLE.—A happy omen of an end to worry and vexation.

FACES.—The importance of such an omen in a dream depends upon whether the Face is smiling or repulsive, for it is a straight dream, and anything coarse or ugly means ill fortune. To dream that you are washing your own Face, shows trouble of your own causing. If the Faces are those of absolute strangers, it shows a change of residence or of occupation.

FACTORY.—A Factory is a sign of some unexpected happening. If the place shows signs of great activity, then the coming change will be all the more important. An idle Factory shows that the change will bring worry and loss.

FAGGOTS.—Bad news.

FAILURE.—This is a dream of contrary, since if you Fail in any attempt in your dream, you will succeed in real life.

FAINT.—It is always a bad omen if you see signs of collapse or illness in your dream, whether you are the sufferer yourself, or whether you tend someone who is ill.

FAIRIES.—This is a very favourable dream, and shows success when least expected.

FAIRS.—It is not fortunate to dream that you are present at a Fair ; beware of rivals in business and love.

FAITHLESS.—A dream of contrary. If you dream that you are false to someone, or they to you, it is a good omen.

FALCON.—You are surrounded by enemies who envy you.

FALL.—To dream that you Fall from a height is a sign of misfortune, and the longer the distance you Fall, the greater will be the coming trouble.

FALSEHOOD or LIE.—Another dream of contrary, whether you are the liar, or whether you dream that someone is telling Lies to you.

FAME.—This is one of the dreams that " go by contraries " and warn the dreamer against failure.

FAMILY.—To dream of a numerous Family is a good sign of prosperous times in store ; also to dream of relatives as long as they are friendly.

FAMINE.—To dream that you have not enough to eat is a contrary dream—you will live in greater comfort.

FAMOUS.—To dream that you have become Famous is a bad sign. It shows loss and change for the worse.

FAN.—Be cautious. This is not actually a bad dream, but a warning that you should not be venturesome.

FAREWELL.—It is generally considered a good sign to dream of bidding good-bye to anyone.

FARM.—To dream that you are engaged in Farm work is a fortunate omen ; it indicates material success, though after some struggle on your part. If you only visit a farm, it indicates good health.

FARTHINGS.—If someone gives you a copper coin, in your dream, it indicates loss of money in some business venture.

FASHIONS.—To dream that you are studying the Fashions, either in a magazine, or in the shop windows, is a sign of some small change, either for good or ill.

FASTING.—Times of good cheer are at hand.

FAT.—To dream that you are growing Fat is an unfortunate sign, especially for a woman.

FATHER.—If, in your dream, you see your Father, and he speaks to you, it is a sign of coming happiness. If he is silent, or if he appears to be ill or dead, then you may expect trouble. See also **MOTHER.**

FATHER-IN-LAW.—To dream you see your Father-in-law, either dead or alive, signifies ill-luck, especially if he uses violence or is threatening.

FATIGUE.—To dream that you are tired is a contrary omen, for it indicates coming success in some venture.

FAULT.—It is a dream of contrary if you do wrong and are reproved by your friends.

FAVOUR.—This is a dream of contrary, for if you dream that someone has done you a Favour, it shows a loss of money in some business transaction.

FAWN or DEER.—This is looked upon as unfavourable, especially where love affairs are concerned.

FEAR.—This dream has many interpretations, as, naturally, it varies so greatly in the circumstances. Fear can be felt and shown in so many forms. Roughly speaking, it should be treated as an obstacle dream. If you overcome your Fears, or get over your trouble, then all will go well. But if the Fear persists, and you cannot trace the cause, then expect treachery or deceit on the part of someone you trust.

FEASTING.—A dream of contrary—expect difficulties in the near future.

FEAT.—To dream of doing great deeds presages failure and humiliation.

FEATHERS.—It is wise to put no meaning to Feathers in themselves ; they should be treated as emblems of colour, such as White, Black, Red, Blue, and so on. See under **COLOUR** for the meaning.

FEATURES.—To dream of a strange face with Features which you can remember on waking indicates important introductions. Blue eyes indicate a new friendship ; dark eyes a lover ; bearded face, a traveller will return ; smiling face, a wish will be granted.

FEEBLE or WEAK.—To dream that you are tired or worn-out is a fortunate omen.

FEEDING.—To dream that you are Feeding animals is an excellent omen. Your affairs will prosper. It is not, however, a good sign to dream that you yourself are feasting.

FEET.—To dream that you bathe your Feet signifies molestation and trouble.

FENCE.—Like all dreams concerning obstacles, this is a sign of difficulties ahead. The result depends upon the upshot of your dream.

FENCING.—To dream of a Fencing match denotes an adventure in which your wits will be your only weapon.

FENDER.—Should you dream you are standing on a Fender, you will soon travel to a foreign country.

FERNS.—If you dream of Ferns in luxurious growth, it is a very favourable omen. Mother Nature is helping you to Success. But if it is Autumn, or if the foliage is decaying for any reason, then accept it as a warning of coming trouble. If the Ferns are in pots, instead of growing naturally in the open, then the success will only come after effort and difficulty.

FERRET.—Be on your guard against spiteful gossip.

FERRY.—Danger is around you. Try to do nothing you do not wish known and do not walk by a river unless necessary.

FESTIVAL.—This has much the same meaning as Feasting—it is not a fortunate omen.

FETTERS or HANDCUFFS.—A dream of coming obstacles. If you are not set free from your chains, then you may expect business difficulties of a serious nature.

FEVER or ILLNESS.—This is generally looked upon as an omen of contrary meaning. If you dream that you are Ill, you can rest assured that your health is good.

FIANCÉ.—A disagreement or argument soon overcome.

FIDDLE or MUSICAL INSTRUMENT.—Music is associated with prosperity in your dreams; it is a good sign. See also **VIOLIN**.

FIELDS.—Fortunate happenings of a personal character —agreeable and pleasant friends, hospitality, and merry-making.

FIEND.—This is an omen very similar to Evil Spirits. It is a serious omen unless you escape from the clutches of the Fiends that are worrying you.

FIFE.—To hear this played indicates travel to see a relative in the Army.

FIGHTING.—Another example of an obstacle dream— the result will depend upon what happens; if you are beaten in the Fight, you must expect misfortune or a love reverse. If you are successful in your dream, then you will overcome your difficulties.

FIGS.—An unexpected and fortunate event.

FIGURES or NUMBERS.—This omen is a difficult one to judge, as the importance of the dream depends upon the Figures involved, and these again depend upon the circumstances of the dream. As a rough guide, low Figures are fortunate, high Figures are bad, while medium, in-between Figures show difficulties that can be surmounted if you exert yourself. Obviously, high Figures for a girl or for a working-man would only be low Figures for the wealthy individual, or prosperous business man, to whom a few thousands would mean little or nothing.

FILE.—To dream you are using a File presages new work.

FILMS.—A possible journey abroad in the near future, much discussion—guard against your tongue.

FINDING.—This is an omen of contrary. The more valuable the article you find, the greater will be your loss in business.

FINGER-POST or SIGN-POST.—An omen of some coming change, though it may only be a fresh house or flat.

FINGERS.—To cut your Finger, or otherwise damage it, is a sign of quarrelling with your friends or family circle.

FIRE.—An omen of warning. If the Fire is small and does no mischief, then expect news of some sort, though not of great importance. If the Fire burns you, then expect a serious mischance in your affairs.

FIRE-ARMS.—A certain indication of a coming quarrel.

FIRE ENGINE.—It is an omen of danger to see a Fire Engine, but its importance depends upon whether it is going to the scene of a fire, or returning. This can be judged by the pace, and by the clanging bell.

FIRESIDE.—A good omen, both for domestic life, and business affairs. A prosperous year is in front of you.

FIREWORKS.—It is a sign of coming treachery if you watch Fireworks in your dream. Be careful in your business transactions and avoid speculations.

FIRMAMENT.—To see the heavens moonlit and starry, is a sign that fortune will favour you especially when travelling.

FIR TREE.—The dark colouring peculiar to Fir Trees suggests the misfortune of Black, softened by the more fortunate toil of the green. Work hard and all will go well ; slacken, and you may expect losses.

FISH.—To dream of Fish swimming freely, is a sign of coming good fortune ; but if you catch them, or see them dead, as in a shop, then expect trouble.

FISHING.—See **FISH,** also **ANGLING.**

FITS.—It is not a good sign to see illness in a dream. See **FAINT.**

FLAGON.—To drink from a Flagon of wine is a foreboding of illness, which you may, however, avoid by careful living.

FLAGS.—There are different interpretations of this omen in various parts of the world, so it is better to ignore it and study instead the other indications in your dream. Some people consider that the generous display of coloured bunting is a fortunate omen. But all colours are not propitious, so this point is doubtful. For instance (see **COLOURS**), Red is generally considered a warning of quarrels with friends, while Black is ominous. There should be plenty of White, Blue, Orange, or Green, if the bunting is to bring good luck.

FLAMES.—As a rule, this is a bad sign, but if the Flames have been got under control, all will come well, though there may be difficulties ahead. See **FIRE ENGINE.**

FLASH.—To dream of a Flash of light, whether from a searchlight or torch is a sign of important news that will cause your plans to succeed.

FLASK.—To dream of drinking wine from a Flask presages the enjoyment of a fortune ; if the wine holds water, you will be happy but not rich ; to break a Flask, losses.

FLATTERY.—This is much the same as Falsehood, for all Flattery is insincere and unreliable. It is a dream of contrary. If someone is Flattering you, then expect trouble or disappointment.

FLEET.—Ships at sea always form a bad omen, and it does not really matter what type of vessels they are ; of course, this does not apply to a shipwreck or other maritime disaster.

FLIES.—Annoyance from small insects, such as **BEES, FLIES, GNATS,** and so on, is a sign of worry and trouble caused by friends and acquaintances.

FLIRTING.—On the whole, a prosperous omen, but not if you carry it to a heartless extent, or cause tears.

FLOATING.—This is a good dream if all goes well—it is really a variation of the obstacle dream. If you sink or find it difficult to keep afloat, then expect trouble ahead.

FLOODS.—This is a good sign for those whose lives bring them in contact with water or the sea ; but for others, it should be treated as an obstacle dream, and is especially unfortunate for love affairs.

FLOOR.—To dream that you are sweeping or washing the Floor is a bad omen for business success. You will not be fortunate, though your losses may not amount to a large sum. To sit or lounge on the Floor, on the contrary, is a very good omen.

FLOUR.—It is not a good omen to buy or to use Flour in the course of your dream.

FLOWERS.—One of the best of Nature dreams, this foretells great happiness, unless you throw away the blossoms, when you will suffer from your own careless actions.

FLUTE.—It is a very fortunate dream if you see yourself playing the Flute—but you may expect difficulties if you see someone else playing this instrument.

FLYING.—Another obstacle dream, the meaning of which depends on the result. But aviation is of such modern growth, that such a dream must indicate ambitious plans, possibly beyond your real power of accomplishing.

FLYING FISH.—Deceitful associates and late hours hold especial danger ; try to avoid both for some time.

FOAL.—You will hear of the birth of a child.

FOAM.—Cheerful scenes will soon surround you.

FOG.—An obstacle dream of great power, especially to those in love—your prospects of happiness are doubtful. If the Fog clears away and the sun shines again, you will get over your disappointment in time.

FOLDING.—It is a good sign for your love affairs if you

dream that you are careful when Folding your clothes or house linen.

FOLIAGE.—If green, pleasures are in store for you. If dead, your undertakings will not succeed.

FONT.—Another dream connected with the inside of a sacred building. It is not a fortunate omen.

FOOD.—It is generally a fortunate sign to eat Food in your dream, provided you are soon satisfied. But it is not a good omen to eat like a glutton.

FOOLISH.—It is a good omen, if in your dream you imagine that you have done some Foolish action.

FOOT or LEG.—Beware of treachery if someone trips you up with his or her foot.

FOOTBALL.—To witness a game of Football is a bad sign. You may expect worries, possibly in connection with some friend. It is a good sign to see yourself playing, provided your side wins, or you yourself score a goal.

FOOTMAN or MANSERVANT.—This is an omen of unexpected trouble for those who are not used to keeping such Servants. Otherwise it can be disregarded.

FOOTPRINTS.—Difficulties which you will soon surmount by your own efforts.

FOOTSTEPS.—You will hear something which will spur you on to greater exertions and success.

FOP.—For a girl to dream of a Foppish man portends a lover of inferior position.

FOREIGN COUNTRY.—Your happiness lies at home.

FOREIGNERS.—To dream of Foreigners is usually considered very fortunate for your love affairs.

FOREST.—Another variation of the obstacle dream. The meaning will depend upon what happens, and whether you emerge from the Forest or Wood.

FORGE.—To see a Blacksmith at work shows troubles over your love affairs. The brighter the glow of the fire, the more the sparks, the more serious the quarrel.

FORGERY.—It is a bad omen to dream that you are guilty of Forgery. But it is a good sign if someone else forges your signature.

FORGET-ME-NOT.—You are beloved and remembered by many.

FORK.—To dream of Forks is a sign of a quarrel.

FORLORN.—To feel Forlorn or Miserable is a bad sign, unless in your dream you regain a cheerful state of mind.

FORSAKEN.—A good omen of the affections of those you dreamed lost.

FORT.—Troubles and losses in store for you.

FORTUNE.—A dream of contrary. The more fortunate and successful you are in imagination, the greater will be your struggles in real life.

FORTUNE TELLING.—It is a most unfortunate omen to have your Fortune told in a dream. But you will ensure success if you tell the Fortune of any other person.

FOSSILS.—You will hear of the sickness of someone you have not met for a long time.

FOUNTAIN.—A good dream if the water is clear.

FOWLS.—To dream of these common domestic Birds shows a commonplace and uneventful life, without ups and downs.

FOX.—To see a Fox in your dream indicates an enemy or a rival among your acquaintances. If you see the animal killed, you will overcome the threatened trouble.

FOXGLOVES.—These bold and handsome flowers are considered a fortunate omen.

FRAGRANCE.—It is a good sign to dream of a pleasant perfume, but the results will not be very serious—some small success is indicated.

FRANTIC.—To dream of being Frantic means a peaceful holiday after strenuous times.

FRAUD.—To dream that someone has cheated you is a sign of treachery; but if you dream that you yourself have committed a Fraud, it shows coming prosperity.

FREEMASON.—To dream of becoming one indicates new friends and far journeys.

FRENCH.—To dream of speaking and hearing foreign languages is a fortunate sign especially in love affairs.

FRETTING.—This brings joyful tidings and explanations of something which has puzzled you.

FRIENDS.—A good omen, for you will receive unexpected good news, unless you dream that they are in trouble.

FRIGHT or FRIGHTENED.—A dream of contrary; the more dreadful your ordeal, the greater your success. Your business affairs will prosper if you persevere, whatever your present difficulties.

FROTH.—A short happiness gained at great cost.

FROGS or TOADS.—Success in business, a good dream.

FROST or BAD WEATHER.—Many troubles ahead of you; be careful what you do in the near future.

FROWN.—This is a dream of contrary. It is a sign of much domestic happiness, or the company and confidence of some friend. It does not concern your business affairs, nor your money matters.

FRUIT.—As with Colours, the meaning of Fruit in your dream varies according to the kind.

Almonds or Nuts show difficulties, but not so great that they cannot be overcome.

Apples are tokens of success and good health.

Apricots or Peaches are very favourable signs especially in love affairs and friendships.

Cherries or Plums show disappointment in domestic affairs, small family quarrels and difficulties.

Currants indicate happiness in married life, a faithful and devoted partner. See **Grapes.**

Elderberries or Wild Fruits indicate difficulties. You may not secure great prosperity, but you will find yourself comfortably placed in business and in home affairs.

Figs are generally considered a foreign fruit, though they are sometimes grown in England. Expect small legacies or unexpected news.

Filberts.—See **Almonds.**

Gooseberries are similar to Currants, and concern your domestic affairs.

Grapes indicate success in business, as well as happiness in your home life. See **Currants**.

Lemons are an omen of family discord or of disappointment in love. See **Oranges**.

Melons show a successful intervention on your part in some trouble among your friends.

Mulberries or Raspberries or Strawberries are favourable for love affairs and domestic happiness.

Nuts.—See **Almonds**.

Oranges indicate business difficulties. See also **Lemons**.

Peaches.—See **Apricots**.

Plums.—See **Cherries**.

Raspberries.—See **Mulberries**.

Strawberries.—See **Mulberries**.

Walnuts.—See **Almonds**.

Wild Fruit.—See **Elderberries**.

FRYING PAN.—To be cooking a meal in your dream is the sign of an unfortunate quarrel.

FUN.—Excessive merriment is a bad sign in a dream, and foretells difficulties in business affairs. The more boisterous your amusement, the more serious matters will be. Quite homely happiness is a different matter.

FUNERAL.—This dream is associated with the colour Black, but if you see yourself present at a funeral in Black it is appropriate, so no harm need be expected. It is a dream of contrary and indicates a successful love affair.

FUNERAL SERVICE.—Inheritance.

FUR or FUR GARMENTS.—A favourable dream on the whole, though it foretells change of some sort.

FURNACE.—This is an omen very similar to Forge in its meaning.

FURNITURE.—This is generally a good dream, but it depends upon circumstances. Handsome Furniture is very fortunate, but naturally, this depends upon the person who dreams. What is ordinary Furniture for a wealthy woman would be sheer folly for a working-class woman, or for a business girl earning her own living.

It should be just a little better in quality than what you actually possess.

FURY.—To dream of a Furious person denotes a reconciliation ; of a Furious animal, a friend defends your name.

FUTURE.—An unusual dream predicting unusual events. You may have the chance to make up an old quarrel or mend an old wrong.

G

GABLE.—Good advice will be given you, which if followed will lead to good fortune.

GAG.—To dream that there is a Gag in your mouth is an obstacle omen. If you do not succeed in getting free, then you may expect serious trouble ahead.

GAIETY.—Like Fun, this is generally a bad omen in a dream.

GAIN.—A sign of contrary. To dream that you are making a big income, or having pulled off a successful business deal, is a bad sign, unless you appear to have scored by cheating, or by taking some unfair advantage.

GAITERS.—A fortunate omen for your love affairs.

GALA.—A change of residence, many servants, a parting from relations is indicated.

GALE.—Better times to come, do not take present vexations too seriously, especially quarrels.

GALLERY.—Worries will soon pass unless you should dream of falling from the Gallery.

GALLOP.—An easy Gallop on a straight road portends success to your plans ; up a steep path warns the dreamer to think well before acting.

GALLOWS.—This unpleasant dream is one that carries a contrary meaning, and is generally considered very fortunate in every way.

GAMBLING.—Do not act on the ideas of others or you will incur loss.

GAME.—To dream that you are taking part in a Game is a mixed omen, for it depends upon the result, for one thing, and after that, it is contrary in its meaning. If you win for yourself, or your side, it is an unfortunate sign and means misfortune in business. But to lose, indicates that you will be prosperous. See also **BIRDS** and **PARTRIDGE.**

GANGWAY.—Should you cross it you have aroused the hostility of a rival. Take care not to lose what is now your own through over-confidence.

GAOL.—An obstacle dream. If you are released, it shows great good fortune, for disgrace, in any form, in a dream is an omen of contrary, so there is a large element of success in spite of your present difficulties.

GARDEN.—A very fortunate dream, Nature at her best, but of course it must be a Garden that is well kept, and not neglected. It concerns money matters.

GARLAND.—See **FLOWERS.**

GARLIC or ONIONS.—These are generally considered fortunate omens. But there are many people who detest the smell of Onions, and in such cases they should be treated as signs of ill-success.

GARROTTER.—To dream of meeting a criminal denotes violent opposition to your opinions. Be firm as you are in the right.

GARRET.—An advancement in position should come speedily.

GARTER.—To dream that you have lost your Garter indicates coming misfortune. If both Garters should be loose and come down, the omen becomes more emphatic. If someone picks it up and returns it to you, it is a sign that a loyal friend will help you in your difficulty ; but if the person retains the Garter, then your troubles will be increased by treachery on the part of someone near you.

GAS or LAMP LIGHT.—This concerns your love affairs or domestic happiness. If you dream that the light is bad, then your interests will suffer accordingly. If the light goes out suddenly, expect a catastrophe.

GATHER or PICK UP.—To dream of Picking up money, is a fortunate sign ; if you are Gathering fruit, it refers to pleasure or enjoyment. Flowers concern love affairs.

GAUZE.—Concealed feelings.

GAVOTTE.—To dream of dancing a Gavotte signifies a calm and happy future.

GAZELLE.—To dream of this gentle-eyed animal, means to a girl a rough wooer but a true husband.

GEMS.—Jewels are not favourable omens in a dream, nor is any excessive display of luxury.

GENTRY.—For a country girl this signifies change of scene. She will work in a large city before long.

GERANIUMS.—These popular garden plants are often seen in dreams. They are not Geraniums really, but that is the popular though incorrect name. They can be taken as omens of variety.

GHOST.—This is only unfortunate if the sight of the Apparition appears to cause fright. Then you may expect a troubling time ahead of you. But if you do not fear the Ghost, you will pull through your difficulties, especially if the Spirit disappears.

GIANT.—One of the many obstacle omens. It signifies difficulties that can be overcome if met boldly, but the result depends on the circumstances of the dream.

GIDDY.—To feel ill or Giddy in your dream is a sign of change, probably for the better. But all changes entail hard work.

GIFT.—A dream of contrary—beware of the person from whom you receive a gift under such circumstances.

GILDING.—A present will be offered to you ; think well before accepting it as the motive behind it may not be that of friendship.

GIN.—To dream of drinking Gin denotes short life and many changes.

GIPSY.—An omen of varying meaning. If the Gipsies offer any of their wares and you buy, it shows good fortune coming to you, but probably after some change, or from a distance.

GIRL.—Surprising news; a reply long delayed will reach you at last.

GLADIATOR.—Something will happen which will cause you sorrow and anguish.

GLASS.—This dream depends upon the details, whether the glass is clear or cloudy. If all is well, it is a fortunate dream, especially in matters of business.

GLEANERS.—A dream indicating prosperity, especially if you yourself should be Gleaning.

GLOBE.—This indicates friends scattered abroad. Several letters from across the water are likely to come.

GLOOM.—A possible change for the better will come your way. Do not hesitate to grasp a chance.

GLOVES.—This omen is very similar to that concerning **GARTERS,** but any good or bad fortune will be short-lived.

GLOW.—An improvement in your fortunes is about to happen, should you dream of a brilliant Glowing scene.

GLOW-WORM.—You will have the chance of doing a great kindness which will well repay you later.

GLUE.—This portends faithful friendship from one whom you trust.

GLUTTON.—You are in danger of poverty; make every effort in your power against it while there is yet time.

GNATS.—Backbiters will cause you loss and trouble.

GOAL.—This presages a postponement but not failure of your hopes.

GOATS.—Many trials, but you will face them bravely. If the animals are White or Black or Piebald, then you must take the colour into consideration, as well. See **BLACK,** also **WHITE,** for a Piebald animal; your luck will be very erratic and unreliable.

GOBLET.—If you dream of drinking out of a Goblet, you will have good times and be happy.

GOD.—To hear His voice or to dream that He speaks to you, happiness and joy.

GOLD.—A dream of contrary as far as the metal itself is concerned, for it signifies loss of money. But if your clothes are of Gold cloth, or if they are embroidered with Gold ornamentation, it is a good sign.

GOLDFISH.—Trouble in business.

GOLDMINE.—To discover one, great and certain gain.

GOOD.—To dream that you do good signifies jollity and pleasure, and to dream that others do good to you means profit and gain.

GOLF.—To dream that you are spending your time playing games, is a warning that your business affairs need attention.

GOLF-LINKS.—To dream of playing this game denotes a busy life at home.

GOOSE.—See **DUCKS.**

GOOSEBERRIES.—See **FRUIT.**

GONDOLA.—This presages a happy but unromantic life.

GONG.—An exciting event in the family. Avoid trifling with important matters.

GORSE.—Good fortune will come your way; try to grasp it.

GOUT.—Avoid overstrain; you are not too strong just at present.

GOVERNMENT.—To dream of a post under Government is an omen of a precarious living and much poverty.

GOWN.—A dream of contrary—the more handsomely you are dressed, the worse the omen. In fact, the most fortunate dream a woman can have is to imagine herself naked. See **EVE.** If, however, your clothes are shabby or torn, it is a fortunate sign, though not so good as nakedness.

GRAIN.—This is a very fortunate omen, although your success will come to you from hard work and endeavour. Persevere and you will be richly rewarded.

GRAMOPHONE.—Pleasant tidings from a distance. An unexpected discovery will be made.

GRANDPARENT.—To dream that you are a Grandparent, or that your grandchildren are present, is a very favourable sign.

GRAPES.—See **FRUIT.**

GRASS.—As in the case of a **GARDEN** this dream is fortunate if the grass is seen green and flourishing—not otherwise.

GRASSHOPPER.—Loss of harvest.

GRATITUDE.—Surprising events will happen to you should you dream of being exceedingly grateful to someone ; but should you dream of another expressing gratitude to you, the events will happen to someone dear to you.

GRAVE.—News from afar. If the Grave space is open, the news will not be good.

GRAVEL.—To dream that you are walking on a rough gravel path is equivalent to an obstacle dream, but naturally it concerns small affairs. If you complete your journey, all will be well.

GREY HAIR or WHITE.—These signs of advancing age are most fortunate, especially if you are in the company of a Grey-haired person in your dream. If you imagine that you yourself are Grey, it is still fortunate, but indicates difficulties before success.

GREENFINCH.—This dream warns you to stick to your work and undertakings if you would avoid loss.

GRENADIER.—For a girl to dream of a Grenadier, denotes a civilian husband in the near future.

GREYHOUND.—You will win more than a race despite keen rivalry.

GRIEF.—This indicates joy and merry times.

GRINDING.—(Corn) good fortune ; (coffee), trouble at home ; (pepper), sickness and sorrow.

GRINDSTONE.—To be using a Grindstone in your dream is an omen of contrary—good fortune will attend your efforts.

GROANS.—It is not fortunate to hear people Groaning in your dreams, unless you assist them.

GROOM.—Legal affairs will be made known to you probably to your advantage.

GROPING.—Your affairs are on the mend, and there is more reason to rejoice than to despair. An introduction will cheer you shortly.

GROTTO.—Your business will improve. To be transported into one indicates a perilous journey.

GROUND.—To dream that you are stretched out on the Ground signifies a humble status for some time to come.

GRUEL.—If you dream of eating it, do not put yourself in the power of anyone who is addicted to strong liquors, or you may have cause to regret it.

GUARD.—To dream of keeping watch against peril of some kind, is a warning to avoid ill-considered speech which may put you in a difficult position.

GUESTS or VISITORS.—Not a fortunate dream. The more visitors who come to you, the greater will be your business difficulties.

GUIDE.—To be Guiding someone else in a dream signifies kindly assistance in your own difficulties from good friends.

GUITAR or BANJO.—This is much the same omen as Violin, and it is a fortunate dream if the music pleases you. Any interruption is a bad sign.

GUM.—Someone will "stick to you" in an emergency. Financial delays are indicated.

GULF.—A sign of a parting which will sadden you. Avoid it if you can.

GUN.—To hear the report of a Gun is an omen of illness concerning some loved one, but it will pass away. If you hear several reports, the illness will last for a longer period. If you yourself fire the Gun, you will be the invalid concerned.

GUNPOWDER.—To a man, this dream means a speedy change of residence ; to a girl, a wedding with a soldier

GUTTER.—To dream of being in the Gutter yourself, denotes hard times to come. Should you find anything valuable in a Gutter, financial reward will come later for hard work done now.

GYMNASTICS.—Any violent exercise is a dream of contrary. Your plans will fail, because you will not be able to put sufficient energy into your work.

H

HABIT.—To dream of putting on, or wearing a Riding-habit, indicates a great effort which you will have to make to escape from some unhappy position. Be brave, as you have more friends than you think you have.

HADDOCK.—Dreaming of fish is generally fortunate.

HAG.—Gossip and scandal about women friends.

HAIL or SNOW.—This is a bad dream and foretells difficulties and disappointment. See also **SNOW**.

HAIR.—If you dream about your personal appearance, it is a sign of continued prosperity if you are satisfied with your image. If your Hair is getting thin or falling out, it is a bad sign. If you worry because your Hair is turning grey, it shows that difficulties are ahead and that your affairs will need careful attention.

HAIRPINS.—A visit to a place of amusement of a novel kind, or to see something which is quite new to you, is indicated.

HALO.—Present pain will lead to good fortune later. Be brave.

HALL.—To dream of a great Hall in a strange place means important decisions to be made shortly.

HALIBUT.—To dream of this fish betokens a meal in public, held in your honour.

HALL MARK.—A double-faced companion is trying to injure your reputation.

HALTER.—A former playmate will become your marriage partner.

HAM.—A fortunate omen, but it concerns trivial matters.

HAMLET.—To dream of a small village or Hamlet indicates a removal to a crowded city.

HAMMER.—Unlike hearing the noise of a gun being fired, it is fortunate if you hear the sound of a Hammer being used. It is a good sign in every way, both for business and love affairs.

HAMMOCK.—This is a sign of a loss, and also of a gain of more value than the loss; probably to do with a lover.

HAMPER.—A pleasant visit is to be paid. Be careful of travelling at a late hour.

HAND.—Another dream that concerns your personal appearance—see also **HAIR.** If your hands are dirty, you should be careful over your affairs, for success is doubtful. If your Hands should be tied, you will have great difficulty in overcoming your troubles. But to dream that you are Shaking Hands with some person is fortunate, for some unexpected event will enable you to put things right.

HANDCUFFS.—This is a dream of contrary—good fortune awaits you.

HANDKERCHIEF.—Someone has a gift for you.

HANDWRITING.—It is not a good sign to see written documents in your dream. Be careful of new or untested ventures.

HANGING.—To dream that you are being Hanged denotes good to you. To dream that you see a person Hanged is an omen of good to him. He will attain wealth and great honour.

HAPPY.—Any excessive pleasure or merry-making in a

dream is an omen of contrary. The more boisterous your pleasures, the greater your business difficulties will prove.

HARBOUR.—Means a happy time to come, with one you care for. Falsehood will be exposed.

HAREBELLS.—To dream of gathering Harebells, bluebells or any blue wildflowers, is an omen of finding a true lover.

HARE or RABBIT.—This is not a good sign. Things will be difficult, but a change of residence or occupation will help to put matters right.

HAREM.—Truth will out. Things you believe unknown are the subject of much gossip, but you will triumph in the end.

HARMONIUM.—To hear this played or play it in a dream signifies a happy but solemn occasion, probably a friend's wedding to which you will be invited.

HARMONY.—All pleasant music is a fortunate omen, but there must not be any sudden stoppage.

HARP.—See **VIOLIN.** All pleasant music is a favourable omen in a dream.

HARNESS.—A pleasant evening and an introduction which will lead to friendship.

HARROW.—To dream of implements is fortunate only if they are those used in your own work, otherwise they indicate dangerous rivals.

HASSOCK.—To dream of a Hassock betokens disappointment if you kneel upon one ; triumph over rivals if you have your feet upon one.

HART or DEER.—To dream of wild animals in captivity is unfavourable, and shows quarrels and losses.

HARVEST.—To dream that you see the workers busy on the Harvest is a most favourable dream—Nature favours you. It is very fortunate for those in love. See also **GRAIN.**

HAT.—New clothes are generally excellent omens, but shabby things are warnings of trouble. If you lose your Hat, beware of false friends.

HATBOX.—To dream of opening one denotes a gay occasion unless you find it empty, in which case it means disappointment about a festivity to which you will not be invited.

HATCHET.—You will be in danger soon. Anxiety and trouble.

HATCHING.—Turn your mind from all unhappy thoughts and look ahead to brighter times amongst friends.

HATRED or MALICE.—A dream of contrary. To Hate anyone in your dream is a sign of success with friends or in your domestic affairs.

HAWK.—Birds of prey are omens of coming losses. Be careful over your business ventures and speculations.

HAWKER.—A new influence is about to enter your life ; be reserved with present associates.

HAWTHORN.—A very favourable omen, as indeed are most Spring blossoms. The colour, White, helps considerably in this case.

HAY.—A very favourable dream. Nature helps you and you should be successful both in business and love.

HAYCART.—Through diligence you will succeed in your undertaking.

HAYSTACK.—Strive on, you have laid the foundation for a prosperous future.

HAZEL-NUT.—Arguments and discussion to come. Try to prevent them from developing into serious quarrels.

HEAD.—Pains in your Head, or dreams about accidents are warnings of difficulties ahead of you. Persevere, but be prudent, and do not take any risks.

HEARSE.—Beware of fire and deceit. Save your pence and trust few people ; you are shortly making an important change.

HEART.—Warm affection is felt for you where you least expect it.

HEARTH.—To be cooking at the fire, you will successfully carve out your own future.

HEAT.—You have no reason to worry over your circumstances, but avoid angry thoughts or words.

HEATHENS.—To dream of going to a savage country amongst Heathens is one of the dreams that " goes by contraries ", and indicates a contented but stay-at-home life.

HEATHER.—A fortunate dream, especially in the case of the white variety, where the colour greatly helps.

HEAVEN.—A dream of Heaven is a sign of prosperity and happiness in this life.

HEAVENS.—It is a fortunate omen when you dream of the skies ; but if there are many clouds about, then expect to face difficulties.

HEDGEHOG.—Your kindness will be taken advantage of.

HEELS.—If wounded there or in pain there, innumerable troubles.

HEDGES.—A green and flourishing Hedge is a good sign. But if in your dream, they are obstacles to your path, then you must expect difficulties, as with all such dreams.

HEIRLOOM.—An answer postponed. Do not be dominated by a friend.

HELL.—There are many interpretations concerning this omen in a dream, but personally we consider it a sign of disturbed health and not a true dream at all.

HELMET.—Pleasant visitors ; avoid extravagance ; you will need all your savings.

HEMP.—Fortune favours you. It indicates luck.

HEN.—A dream of commonplace affairs. But if you see the Hens laying eggs, you may expect good luck. Chickens, however, are not considered fortunate.

HERBS or PLANTS.—Signs of good fortune in almost any case, as they are favoured by Nature. But they must be growing vigorously. If Flowers are seen, it is a very good sign.

HERO.—A change of heart in someone who has hitherto been cool to you, especially should you dream of some great Hero of historic times.

HERMIT.—Sorrow.

HERRING.—Fish are always good omens; you may expect success in business, but you will have to work steadily in order to secure it.

HICCOUGH.—To dream you have a fit of Hiccoughing predicts travel; to dream a friend has it means a parting.

HIDE.—To dream that you are Hiding shows that bad news will soon reach you.

HIGHLAND COSTUME.—It is a favourable dream to see anyone, man or woman, wearing the kilts.

HIGHWAYMAN.—Astonishing information which will be to your advantage.

HILLS.—These must be looked upon as obstacles. If you succeed in climbing the Hill, you will put things right with perseverance. The easier the assent, the better for your future.

HIPS and HAWS.—Poverty or loss of money, especially if you dream you are eating these.

HIVE.—Dangerous undertakings which you will bring to a successful conclusion.

HOARDING.—Be on guard against misfortune through deceitful companions. Your affairs will improve before long.

HOARSENESS.—A chance of advancement but to an insecure position. Think well before deciding.

HOBBY.—To dream of practising your favourite Hobby predicts gains through your own brainwork and efforts.

HOE.—If you are using it in a dream, decide to put up with your present cause of discontent, circumstances will be much improved before long.

HOGS.—If they appear well-fed you have prosperity to come; if they are thin, prepare for bad times.

HOLE.—To creep into one or to fall into one, you will come into contact with undesirable people.

HOMICIDE.—Misfortune and heavy loss.

HOLLY.—A prickly plant—beware of vexations

HOME.—To dream of your old Home or School indicates continued prosperity, especially to the lover.

HONEY.—If you eat Honey, it is a good sign. As the Bees are industrious, so must you be, and then you will thrive.

HONEYMOON.—Changes, journeys and disappointments.

HONEYSUCKLE.—If in flower you will soon change your residence for a fairer scene.

HONOURS.—To dream that you are receiving Honours is an omen of contrary. Be careful or you will lose money.

HOOKS.—A present will soon be given you which you will value greatly.

HOOP.—To dream of anything of a circular nature, such as a Hoop, is a fortunate sign.

HORSE.—These animals are generally good signs, but the colour must be noted, such as Black, White, Brown, and so on. This affects the omen. If you are riding a Horse and are thrown, it is a bad sign. If someone on Horseback comes to visit you, expect news from a distance. It is very lucky to dream of a horse being shod.

HORNS.—To dream one has horns on his head signifies dignity, dominion and grandeur.

HORNETS.—A spiteful rival will seek to injure you ; be on your guard.

HORSESHOE.—To find one indicates a legacy ; to see one, travel over land and water.

HOPPING.—Joy and peace to come ; try not to hurt the feelings of one you care for.

HOTHOUSE or GREENHOUSE.—Good omens as a rule, unless there is much show or " swank " about it. A good deal depends on the Ferns and Flowers seen.

HOUNDS.—These do not form a favourable dream, but shows that any success will only come after much struggle and hard work. See **DOG.**

HOUSE.—A most fortunate omen to see a House being built, but take warning if you see one being pulled down.

HUNGER.—A dream of contrary, for to be Hungry in your dream is a sign of prosperity, but only through hard work and much effort on your part.

HUNTING.—If you are Hunting small animals, such as Hares, it is a sign of disappointment. But if you Hunt a Stag, it is an omen of coming prosperity. The dream of Hunting a Fox, however, shows a risk from clever competition; if you are present at the kill, then you will conquer all difficulties.

HOROSCOPE.—To dream of a chart of your starry influences is a sign that a stronger mind than yours will dominate you, unless you resist with all your might.

HOSPITAL.—A warning to alter ways of living, which lead to ill-health, or a serious misfortune may befall you.

HOTEL.—It is not a favourable sign to dream that you are staying at a fashionable Hotel. Any omens of luxury are bad signs. For a wealthy person, the dream would carry no particular meaning—it is the sense of luxury that means disaster to your plans.

HUMMING BIRDS.—Travel to a foreign clime and successful business there.

HUNCHBACK.—A period of many trials and changes to come, to be followed by a happy love affair.

HURDLES.—Injustice and wrong accusations; you must clear yourself of false suspicions. You will hear of an old acquaintance again.

HURRY.—Danger of fire or accident. Care will avert it.

HURRICANE.—A most unfortunate dream, both for business and for your home life. Be very careful of your actions.

HURT.—A dream of warning, the result depends upon the nature of the accident and whether you recover from it.

HUSBAND.—An omen of contrary in the case of lovers, for if you dream that you are married, when you are not, then expect a quarrel with one dear to you.

HUSSAR.—Unreturned affection will be your fate unless you alter your mind about a civilian lover.

HYACINTH.—You will hear of the misfortune of others, probably sickness.

HYDROPHOBIA.—Robbery and losses; guard your treasures.

HYMNS.—To dream that you are singing Hymns is a fortunate omen; your plans will be successful.

HYSTERICS.—Be firm and do not yourself allow to be dominated by others if you would achieve success.

I

ICE.—This is always an unfortunate dream; expect many difficulties.

ICEBERG.—Every trial will be made of your strength; make a big effort and you will triumph.

ICICLES.—Good luck, happiness and success in love.

IDIOT.—It is a good omen to dream of Idiots; some unexpected good fortune awaits you.

IDLENESS.—A dream of contrary. You will have to work hard if you wish for success in your business ventures.

IDOLS.—Your eyes are about to be opened, do not show your feelings too plainly.

IGNORANCE.—To dream that you are Ignorant, or cannot understand some matter, is an omen of contrary. Success will crown your efforts.

ILLNESS.—A warning of some great temptation that will not work out favourably for you, however promising it appears at first. See also **ACHE** and **DISEASE.**

ILLUMINATION.—Great good fortune. To a lover, it is quite exceptionally fortunate.

IMAGE.—Not a fortunate dream, postpone important decisions.

IMPS.—Grief and disappointment.

IMPALE.—To see anyone Impaled upon railings is a warning of threatened injury to yourself. Be careful.

INCENSE.—It is considered a favourable omen if the Incense is pleasant to your senses, as in the case of all perfumes. But Incense is so closely associated with the interior of a church that we are inclined to treat it doubtfully ourselves, and suggest that success will only come after effort and anxiety.

INCOME.—To dream that you possess a comfortable Income is an unfavourable omen.

INCOME-TAX.—Financial losses, probably through assisting a friend.

INDIA.—Strange happenings; a message of an unfriendly woman.

INDIGO.—A journey over water as blue as this dye, and perhaps a long time before you return.

INDIGENCE.—This dream is often the forerunner of good fortune; a woman will inherit wealth, a man will earn it.

INFANT.—Children are good omens in a dream, but a helpless baby is generally looked upon as a warning of coming trouble.

INFIRM.—It is a dream of contrary if you imagine yourself Aged and Infirm. Old age is a good omen.

INFIRMARY.—A sign of some coming misfortune, if you dream that you are in a hospital. If you recover and leave, you will overcome your difficulties.

INJURY.—To dream that you have been Injured by someone shows that you have a rival, in business or love, who will prove a danger to you.

INK.—If you spill Ink in your dream, expect separation from friends. But to be writing, and using Ink, is a good sign.

INN.—It is generally a good sign to be present at some festivity, but this does not apply to an Inn or Hotel.

INQUEST.—To dream of being at an Inquest denotes prosperity.

INSANITY.—A dream of contrary—your plans will prove successful.

INSECTS.—The interpretation of a dream concerning Insects depends on the circumstances. If the Insects fly or crawl away from you, it is considered that a disappointment awaits the dreamer in his business affairs.

INSOLENCE.—If anyone is Insolent to you in your dream, it is considered a favourable sign. But if you are insolent or cheeky to some other person, then expect difficulties ahead.

INSTRUCTION.—To dream of giving Instructions means that friends will seek your aid; to receive it indicates that you will need sympathy from your friends and a rival will soon win the prize you desire.

INSULT.—A dream of difficulty, the result depending upon what happens. If someone Insults you and you do not resent it, beware of trouble ahead. There may be a change of residence or of occupation.

INTEMPERANCE.—To indulge to excess either in Eating or in Drinking foretells trouble. It is equally as bad to see someone else doing this.

INTESTINES.—Sickness and anxiety.

INUNDATION.—Expect losses of all kinds.

INVALID.—This is best treated as an obstacle dream. If you recover from your illness, then all will go well; if not, you must expect to find difficulties in the path of your success.

INVISIBLE.—A warning of discovery; avoid questionable company and their ways.

INVITATIONS.—Written or printed documents are not good omens in dreams.

INVULNERABLE.—Another warning. Avoid danger to health by every means possible.

IRON.—Most metals indicate difficulties when they are prominent in a dream, but the colour may be held to affect this. Silver or Gold would carry the significance of White or Yellow, whereas Iron would be similar to Black.

IRONING.—A change for the better. Keep yourself free from ties and responsibilities for a time. Help will come to you in an unexpected way.

IRON MOULD.—For a woman to dream of Iron Mould marks on her household linen is a portent of illness in the family.

ISLAND.—Another omen of difficulties ahead, but if you get away from the Island, you will conquer in the end.

ITCH.—Your fears and anxieties are groundless.

IVORY.—A very fortunate dream when Ivory is concerned.

IVY.—Good health awaits you, unless the Ivy is pulled away from its support.

J

JACKASS.—Donkeys are fortunate omens in dreams, and generally concern your love affairs, or married life.

JACKDAW.—An omen of Black. But you will overcome your difficulties if you catch the bird, or if it is in a cage.

JACKAL.—Some enemy will back-bite you and cause you trouble.

JACK.—To dream of playing cards and holding the Jack of Clubs, a good friend ; of Diamonds, a false friend ; of Hearts, a true lover ; of Spades, an enemy.

JACKET.—Hard work and little reward. Be patient, but take the first opportunity of a change.

JACOBEAN.—To dream of Jacobean furnishings presages a quiet time with elderly people whose ways are not so modern as yours, but you will gain by the experience.

JADE.—To dream of Jade ornaments is a fortunate omen, though the colour, green, indicates hard work in front of you if you wish to succeed.

JAIL.—This is generally considered an unfortunate dream, unless you are released in due time. See **JUDGE.**

JARS.—It is considered a good omen to dream of Jars, whether they contain anything or are empty.

JAUNDICE.—Sickness and poverty.

JAW.—It is a bad omen if you dream of any injury to your Jaw; but if you recover, then all will go well after you have conquered the initial difficulties.

JAY.—Difficulties which it will take your utmost efforts to surmount.

JEALOUS.—To dream that you yourself are Jealous of some other person is a bad sign—difficulties of your own making are shown. To dream that someone else is Jealous of you, shows that their attempts to defeat you will turn to your advantage.

JEERS.—To dream of being Jeered at by companions foretells triumph over enemies.

JELLY. It is unfortunate to dream that you are eating Jelly. It is a sort of contrary omen, showing serious difficulties to be tackled.

JELLY-FISH.—A scheme is on foot to injure you; be on guard.

JEOPARDY.—If you dream you are in Jeopardy, it will be very fortunate for you.

JESSAMINE.—It is great good fortune to dream of this beautiful and welcome blossom.

JET.—This black ornament carries no good fortune, and must be judged by its colour alone.

JETTY.—You will travel shortly to another country.

JEWELS.—Always a very fortunate dream, especially for lovers. The omen is just as good whether you give the Jewels to someone else or receive them yourself.

JEW'S HARP.—To dream you see one, indicates good news of a reconciliation. If you play one, the news will affect business relations with an important personage.

JIG.—To dream you are dancing portends at least one lover; be careful not to cause jealousy.

JINGLE.—To hear the Jingle of small bells, either cattle bells, dog bells or sleigh bells, foretells innocent flirtations and amusements.

JOCKEY.—If a woman dreams she sees a Jockey riding at full speed, she will have an unexpected offer of marriage.

JOINT.—A good omen if you cook it for your family, but threatened poverty if you eat it yourself.

JOKER.—Light company will bring you no good; seek your equals.

JILTED.—A dream of contrary—expect good luck in your wooing and happiness in your married life.

JOLLITY.—Too much enjoyment in your dreams is a bad omen. Be careful of your speculations or you will lose heavily.

JOURNEY.—A change in your circumstances is shown, but the details of the Journey will show the result. If your voyage is a pleasant one, all will be for the best; but if the road is rough, or the weather stormy, then be careful.

JOY.—A sign of good health when you are happy in your dreams.

JUBILEE.—To dream you are at a Jubilee is a sure sign that you will have a fortune left you by some rich relations.

JUDGE.—An obstacle dream. It denotes trouble and difficulty ahead, unless the Judge takes your side of the case, in which event, you will pull through in time.

JUGS.—It is a favourable omen if you break a Jug in your dream; but it is considered unfortunate to drink out of a Jug in preference to a glass.

JUGGLER.—An advancement in position will come within your grasp. Do not hesitate.

JUMPING.—Another of the many obstacle dreams. You will meet difficulties, but will overcome them if you persevere.

JURY.—It is considered unfortunate to dream that you form one of a Jury. But if you merely dream that you see the Jury from the Court, then you will overcome your difficulties.

JUNGLE.—Financial affairs will cause you anxiety. Economise while there is time.

JUNIPER.—Someone will speak evil of you. This dream warns you to be circumspect in all your dealings.

K

KALEIDOSCOPE.—Frivolity. Do not take things too lightly or you may regret it.

KANGAROO.—The hostility of someone influential will cause you great anxiety.

KEEL.—To dream of the heavier parts of a ship, such as the Keel, or deck, signifies news of a lover at sea.

KEEPER.—To dream of a Game-keeper or Park-keeper means danger in love matters; a rival will take your place in your sweetheart's affections.

KEEPSAKE.—A dream of good fortune, very similar in meaning to **JEWELS.** But if a friend asks for a Keepsake or a gift, and you fail to respond, then your difficulties will be severe.

KEG.—Filled with liquid, a bad sign in business; with fish, prosperity; empty, a change of surroundings.

KENNEL.—You will be invited to the house of a man you know well. Do not go alone, and avoid quarrels.

KERB.—It is unfortunate to step off the Kerbstone in your dream. Beware of quarrels with friends and relatives.

KETTLE.—A very happy omen if the Kettle is bright

and clean; troubles and losses if the water boils over.

KETTLEDRUM.—Trouble and anxiety.

KEYHOLE.—It is not a good sign to peep through the Keyhole in your dream, or to see someone else spying in this way. Losses will follow quarrels.

KEYS.—To dream that you lose a Key is a bad sign. To give a Key to someone shows good fortune in home life.

KHAKI.—Anxieties are around you, but will be speedily dispersed.

KICK.—It is a bad omen to be Kicked in your dream, for you will have many powerful adversaries. But it is a good omen if you Kick some other person.

KID.—An addition to the family, who will in time bring happiness to the home.

KIDNAPPING.—Your circumstances are about to improve and many of your worries are needless.

KINDLING.—Be careful with tools; you are in danger of accidents. Your love affair will end happily.

KING.—To dream of Royalty is a very favourable sign, unless the Royal person shows signs of displeasure.

KINGFISHER.—To dream of the flash of a blue bird across water signifies a change of luck. If fate has seemed against you, good fortune will befall.

KISS.—This is a fortunate omen provided you have a right to Kiss the person; otherwise your own ill-judged actions will cause your downfall.

KITCHEN.—News from a distance, generally a good omen unless the Kitchen is very bare or untidy.

KITE.—This omen depends on the circumstances. If the Kite flies easily, you may expect success, and the higher up it goes, the better the omen.

KITTEN.—A favourable dream, unless you hurt the young creature.

KNAPSACK.—An obstacle dream, unless you feel no strain from carrying it on your shoulders. But at best, it means difficulties ahead for a time.

KNAVE, AT CARDS.—Trouble and quarrels.

KNEE.—Any injury to your Knee should be treated as an obstacle dream. If it is not serious, then you will come through all right.

KNEEL.—To dream of praying on your Knees is an omen of happiness to come.

KNELL.—Bright and joyful times are in store for you.

KNICK-KNACKS.—Small ornaments and domestic articles are certain indications of domestic troubles and unhappiness.

KNIFE.—Quarrels with friends, that will lead to much misfortune.

KNITTING.—Your undertakings will be crowned with success. If you see someone Knitting you will be deceived.

KNOCKING.—Guard your tongue and you are well on the way to happiness.

KNOTS.—You will meet with much to cause you anxiety.

KNUCKLE.—Should you dream you knock with your Knuckles, unrequited affections.

KURSAAL.—A journey to a new home across the sea. Letter or news from distant relations.

L

LABEL.—Fixing a Label on a box or trunk, shows that you may expect a surprise.

LABORATORY.—Danger and sickness.

LABOURER.—Increased wealth.

LABURNUM.—Ill-natured gossip about you caused by jealousy.

LABYRINTH.—You will unravel some mystery.

LACKEY.—Unexpected joy lies before you.

LACE.—A dream of contrary—the more a woman is decked out in your dream, the greater the coming trouble.

LADDER.—Climbing up a Ladder is a good sign, but the reverse is an indication of troubles ahead of you. The number of rungs should be noted, for this increases the power of the omen. To feel dizzy when on a Ladder is always a bad sign.

LADLE.—Using a Ladle in your dream indicates news from an absent friend.

LAKE.—This dream depends entirely upon the condition. If the water is smooth, and sailing or rowing is pleasant, then you may expect comfort in your home life and success in business. If the weather is stormy or unpleasant, then you are faced with difficulties, which you may overcome with patience and industry.

LADYBIRD.—Good luck in a small venture.

LAMB.—A dream of similar importance to that of playing with a **KITTEN**; it signifies good fortune, unless you spoil your luck by your own action. A Lamb particularly concerns your home life.

LAME.—An omen of business troubles if you find yourself Lame or see a Lame person in your dream. The result will depend upon what happens, and it can be classed as one more of the obstacle dreams.

LAMENT.—This is a dream of contrary. You will hear good news or carry out some favourable business transaction. It does not matter whether you yourself Lament, or whether you dream that someone else is sorrowing.

LAMPS.—See **ILLUMINATION.** This is a fortunate omen, but the result can only be foretold by studying the circumstances of your dream. If the light is dim, you will have to work hard and face difficulties if you wish to succeed. But if there are many Lamps, then your path will be an easy one. If the light goes out, then expect ill-health, or the failure of your plans.

LANDING.—To dream of Landing from a boat portends ill-luck from one associated with the sea.

LANDSLIP or LANDSLIDE.—A short and pleasant visit payed to places once well-known to you.

LAND.—A good dream if you possess Land and retain it ; but if in your dream you move away, then expect a change of occupation, not necessarily for your good. If the owner of the Land orders you away, then expect bitter disappointment.

LANDLADY or LANDLORD.—This is not a favourable dream, and indicates domestic trouble.

LANDSCAPE.—This dream depends upon the circumstances. If the Landscape is a fine open one, that gives you pleasure, then it is a most fortunate dream. But if the view is shut out or obscured by hills or forests, then you will have to face many troubles and obstacles.

LANTERN.—This is usually a fortunate omen, but the light must be good. If it is dim, or if it goes out altogether, then expect worries and difficulties.

LARD.—You will triumph over your enemies.

LARDER.—Expect happiness and a joyful time.

LARKS.—It is one of the best omens possible to hear a bird singing happily ; it is Nature in her kindest mood. But if the songster is shut up in a cage, then your own greed will cause the failure of your plans.

LASH.—To dream of being thrashed, or of thrashing someone else is a warning of trouble over someone you love.

LATE.—To dream of being Late means that your opinions will be asked.

LAUGHING or LAUGHTER.—A dream of contrary, and it is especially serious if you Laugh immoderately or without good cause. Be careful with your love affairs for Laughter in a dream means tears and sorrow in your life.

LAURELS.—These handsome shrubs are fortunate omens, and often indicate money from relatives, or some unexpected gift from a friend.

LAUNDRY.—A sign of a quarrel, parting or loss.

LAVENDER.—An omen as pleasant as it smells.

LAWN.—To dream you see a smooth, green Lawn portends prosperity and well-being, but should you walk on it, the meaning is anxiety.

LAWN TENNIS.—You will find work in which you will take the utmost interest.

LAW, LAWSUIT, or LAWYER.—An omen of serious business troubles ahead of you. Do not start upon any fresh or hastily-considered plan, for the stars do not foretell your success. Do not lend money, for you will not receive it again, nor should you spend too freely after such a dream.

LAZY.—To dream of idling denotes trouble to those near to you affecting you indirectly. A legal matter will end in marriage.

LEAD.—See **IRON,** where it is explained that the significance of metals depends largely upon the general colour. Lead is not a fortunate dream, so be careful and consider your plans once again before you act. To the married, it is a sign of domestic squabbling.

LEAF or LEAVES.—To see trees in full Leaf in your dream is a very happy omen. Your affairs will prosper ; Nature is favourable. It is a very good dream for lovers, especially if Blossom is seen in addition to the Leaf. With Fruit, it is a sign of a happy marriage. But if the Leaves are withered, or are falling, as in Autumn, it shows loss in business, disappointment in love, and domestic affairs, quarrels with friends.

LEAKAGE.—You are wasting your time ; find a wider scope for your activities.

LEAP YEAR.—Frivolity in matters that should be taken seriously.

LEAPING.—See **JUMPING.** Another obstacle dream, the full meaning of which depends upon the circumstances. If you surmount the obstacle, your plans will succeed. To those in love it foretells trivial disagreements, or possible rivals, if the obstacle is a serious one.

LEARNING.—To dream that you Learn something readily is a good sign, but if it proves a difficult task, then you are undertaking more than you can carry through.

LEASE.—If you dream that you are taking a house or a shop, or some land on Lease, it is a very fortunate omen, both in business matters and in love affairs. See also **LAND.**

LEATHER.—It is an unfortunate omen when you dream of Leather in any form, whether as a strap, a bag, harness, or anything else.

LECTURE.—You will soon be in handsome surroundings for a time, but your plans will not wholly succeed.

LEECH.—Fortunate ; friends and happiness await you.

LEDGER.—All written documents or books are unfavourable omens in a dream—this includes Bookkeeping, or the use of Ledgers or Cash Books.

LEEKS.—Perseverance will be necessary if you wish to succeed in your undertakings.

LEFT-HANDED.—A dream portending triumph to all those who are naturally so.

LEGACY.—It is always a fortunate sign to dream that you receive a Legacy or a gift ; but naturally the extent of the good fortune will depend entirely upon the nature of the Legacy.

LEGS.—To dream that you have bruised or injured your Leg foretells money difficulties, which will last for a short or a long period according to the seriousness of the mishap.

LEMONS.—See **FRUIT.** They are not fortunate omens, unless you see them growing on the trees, when it is a sign of an important journey, which will affect your affairs seriously.

LENDING.—A dream of contrary. If you appear to be Lending money or other articles, it foretells that you will want before long. It is an omen of loss and poverty.

LEOPARDS.—Difficulties and dangers are ahead of you. It is probable that you will go abroad on business.

LEPROSY.—This signifies that it is in your power to overcome your worries.

LESSONS.—A sign of good fortunes of every kind.

LETTERS.—To dream that you receive a Letter, is a sign of unexpected news ; but if you post or send a Letter, then you will meet some unexpected difficulty that will upset your plans, but may not cause any real loss. Letters are a sign of something unexpected.

LETTUCE.—Difficulties ahead that can be overcome by prompt and vigorous action on your part.

LIBEL.—A dream of contrary. The more severely you are Libelled in your dream, the greater your success in life.

LICENCE.—A change of occupation will lead you to better things.

LICE.—To dream of Lice and that you are killing a great number of them is a very good omen.

LICKED.—To dream of an animal Licking you denotes that a friend looks at you for guidance.

LIE or FALSEHOOD.—It is a bad omen to dream that you are telling Lies, as your coming troubles will be due to your own misconduct. See **PERJURY.**

LIFT.—Uncertainty. To dream that you are ascending in the Lift, your success is probable ; if descending, it is doubtful.

LIFEBOAT.—This wonderful vessel is an omen of contrary in a dream. If you see it on shore, then expect difficulties ; if you watch it at sea, saving life, then all will be peaceful and quiet in your business affairs.

LIGHT.—See **LAMP,** and also **LANTERN.** A good sign unless the Light goes out or becomes obscured, when it shows difficulties in store for you.

LIGHTHOUSE. -This is a very fortunate dream, and is not often encountered.

LIGHTNING.—This also is a favourable dream, though you will have to face worries, as indicated by the dark clouds from which Nature's unexpected Light is poured. Persevere and you are certain of success.

LILY.—Happiness and prosperity await you, but only as the result of your own industry. Do not expect help from others; you must depend on your own exertions. If, in your dream, the flowers wither, or if you throw them away, then your own thoughtless action will cause your downfall.

LILAC.—Conceit. Do not think too much of appearances, either in yourself or in others.

LIME.—To dream of a heap of Lime indicates a small property soon to be left you.

LIMP.—This is an obstacle dream. If you are forced to rest and cannot complete your journey, then the signs are more favourable for business ventures or speculation.

LINEN.—To dream that you are dressed in clean Linen is a favourable sign; you may expect good news before long. If your Linen is soiled or stained, it denotes serious loss in business, unless you see yourself change the garment, when you may expect to get over your worst difficulties. A dream of Linen also depends upon the colour of the garment—see **WHITE, BLUE,** and other shades under **COLOUR.**

LION.—This dream is not the same in significance as if you see a **LEOPARD.** The Lion signifies some purely personal honour or success, not necessarily involving a gain of money. But if you hear the Lion roaring, as if angry, then expect some misfortune through the jealousy of someone near you. A Lion Cub is a sign of a valuable friendship.

LIONESS.—Dreaming of seeing a Lioness is good to the rich or poor.

LIQUORS.—Drinking freely in a dream shows a change of circumstances, and the other surroundings will decide whether this is in your favour or otherwise.

LOAD.—If you dream that you are heavily laden, it is a certain omen of disaster, probably through your own excessive confidence and lack of careful planning. If you are able to carry the Load without breaking down, then you will pull through.

LINDEN or LIME TREES.—An avenue of Linden trees is an omen of a happy romance near at hand.

LINT.—To dream of binding up a wound with Lint is a warning not to be unforgiving, or you will regret it.

LINTEL.—A sign of a change of residence to a larger home.

LIPS.—To dream that one hath handsome Lips is a sign that your friends enjoy their health. To have them dry and chapped, the contrary.

LIQUEUR.—Beware of flattery.

LISPING.—Be warned against insincerity in a friend, should you dream of hearing someone Lisp.

LITTLE.—To dream you are Little in size or height, you will rise high in life.

LIVER.—To eat it, good health.

LIVERY.—To a servant this indicates success. To a master or mistress it foretells annoyance.

LITTER.—To dream of a Litter of pigs, signifies a fine family ; of other animals, home worries which will however, soon pass.

LIZARD.—Treachery.

LOBSTER or CRAB.—Both these are favourable omens for your love affairs, or your domestic happiness.

LOCKS.—This is another obstacle dream, and you will encounter difficulties in the near future. If cabinets or drawers are Locked and you cannot find the keys, it is a bad sign, and you should be very careful in money matters and avoid speculation or risk of any kind. If later, you find the keys, you will pull through, but even then, it should be taken as a warning. See **KEYS.**

LOCOMOTIVE.—To dream of a Railway Engine is a certain sign of travel, or the arrival of some friend— this depends upon whether the Engine is travelling from you or towards you. If you find yourself burdened with luggage, it becomes an obstacle dream ; if your baggage is light and easy to handle, then your difficulties will be overcome easily. See also **LUGGAGE.**

LOCUST.—Your happiness will be short-lived.

LOCKJAW.—You will marry a nagging partner.

LODGINGS.—To dream you are hunting for Lodgings signifies delay in a matter of importance.

LOGS.—Logs of wood, or the fallen trunks of trees are favourable omens in your dreams; but you must not interfere with them or cut them up.

LONELY.—Feeling alone in a dream is a favourable omen, but it shows that you must depend on your own exertions, not on the influence or help of friends or strangers.

LONGING.—Reconciliation with a former friend.

LOOKING DOWN OR UP.—To dream of Looking Down from a height, such as a hill or a window of a house, shows that you are ambitious and have restless desires. Be careful not to over-reach yourself in your schemes. But if you Look Upwards, then go ahead with all confidence.

LOOM.—Small financial losses followed by improvement in financial matters.

LOOPHOLE.—You have the ability to see far ahead of you and this will aid you in attaining your wishes.

LOOKING-GLASS.—It is a warning that all is not well, when you look into a mirror in your dream. Be careful in your business transactions. Your staff is not supporting you properly, and changes are advisable. To a lover, it shows that the sweetheart is not really faithful. Do not be led away by soft speeches or flattery, but find out the real motive under the surface.

LORD or LADY.—To dream that you are speaking to a Lord, or some person in high authority, signifies social success, but not necessarily a monetary gain. It is purely personal. See **KING**.

LORRY.—Guard your speech or you will lose by it. A chance meeting will bring fortunate results.

LOSING or LOST.—This omen depends largely upon the nature of the article Lost, apart from being an obstacle dream, indicating difficulty ahead, unless you soon find the missing article. It is a sign of domestic trouble if a woman dreams that she has Lost her weddin ring. To dream that you have Lost your shoes, or some other important article of clothing is very unfortunate, for your troubles will be due to your own attempts at being too clever.

LOTTERY.—To dream that you are interested in a Lottery, or hold a ticket for such a Chance, is a bad omen for lovers. There will be an unhappy attachment, or an engagement to some person who will not be worthy of your love.

LOTTO.—To play this game, agreeable company.

LOVE.—This is a dream of contrary as far as sweethearts are concerned. To dream that you do not succeed in Love is a sign that you will marry and have a happy life. But to dream that your friends are fond of you is a very fortunate omen and indicates prosperity. To dream that you are in the company of your Lover is also fortunate.

LOVE-LETTER.—Unpleasant explanations have to be made, and a great deal will rest upon your decision. Remember that frankness is an admirable quality.

LOVE-TOKEN.—A love affair in which you will be greatly interested. Several others know more about it than you think ; be circumspect.

LUCKY.—This is an omen of contrary, for if you dream that you are Lucky in business, or in love affairs, it is an unfortunate sign. Be cautious and use your brains ; do not trust to your affections.

LUGGAGE.—A dream that signifies difficulties in your path, though it depends upon the quantity of Luggage you have with you, and whether you are able to deal with it successfully. For the lover, it foretells quarrels, slight or important according to circumstances.

LUMBER.—Trouble and misfortune.

LUNATIC.—Surprising news which will lead you to different surroundings.

LUXURY.—Another dream of contrary meaning, for the more luxurious your surroundings in your vision, the greater the difficulties and troubles you will have to face. You are not likely to be successful in business, and will probably lose money through bad debts. In love, it foretells a rival, who will probably supplant you. To the married, it shows domestic and family quarrels and trouble.

LYING or FALSEHOOD.—It is a bad omen to dream that you are telling Lies, as your coming trouble will be due to your own misconduct. See **PERJURY**.

LYNX.—You will discover the secret enmity of some person.

M

MACEBEARER.—Dignities and distinctions will be bestowed on you.

MACHINERY.—This dream depends upon whether you feel interested in the Machinery; if so, it is a favourable sign, though it means hard work. But if you feel afraid of the Machinery, then be careful in your ventures, for you will surely fail to carry out your purpose.

MACKEREL.—See **FISH**.

MADNESS.—To dream that you are Mad, or in the company of insane people is a good sign; you will prosper in your affairs. It is a good omen for everyone—those in bad health, those in love, or the business man and speculator.

MACKINTOSH.—To dream of putting it on, portends passing anxieties.

MAD DOG.—Falsehood will be unmasked and unfair accusations proved. A contented future is augured.

MAELSTROM.—Difficulties and bewilderments which will trouble you greatly, but be overcome in the end.

MAGAZINE or BOOK.—Printed papers are not favourable omens in a dream. Be careful if you would avoid loss.

MAGIC.—To dream of things happening by supernatural or unknown means is a sign that changes are coming in your affairs, through some unexpected source. The ultimate result, fortunate or otherwise, will depend upon the details of your dream, but as a rule, the result will be beneficial. But the unexpected happening may mean the loss of a friend, or some event that appears at the time to be unfortunate.

MAGGOT.—A dispute in the home.

MAGISTRATE.—To dream that you are being charged with some crime or offence depends upon whether you are convicted or set free. If convicted, fortune is against you.

MAGNET.—Personal success and security in business. Be careful not to trust too recklessly.

MAGNIFYING-GLASS.—You are apt to "make mountains out of molehills." Meet your worries confidently and they will soon be ended.

MAGPIE.—A bird that combines the forces controlled by both colours, Black and White—see under **COLOUR.** It refers particularly to domestic life or marriage.

MAID.—To dream of a girl is a sign of disappointment, but not if the girl is your own Maidservant.

MALICE.—This is a good dream, and the greater the Malice you encounter in your dream, the better it will be for you.

MALT.—A sign of marriage and much domestic joy.

MAMMOTH.—Apparently unsurmountable obstacles confront you, but your best efforts will assuredly overcome them.

MANGLE.—Indicates assistance from a good friend, but separations from relatives.

MANNA.—A fortunate dream. Approaching money.

MAN.—It is a fortunate omen to dream of a strange Man, but not of a strange woman.

MANICURE.—A marriage with a much older partner will prove a happy one.

MANACLES or HANDCUFFS.—An obstacle dream. If you are set free, all will be well in the end.

MANSERVANT.—See **FOOTMAN.**

MANSION.—All luxury dreams are bad omens. The greater the apparent prosperity, the worse your troubles will be.

MANSLAUGHTER.—See **MAGISTRATE.** But this dream is more serious, and foretells family troubles and disagreements, whatever the ultimate issue may be. It is an unfortunate omen, even though you are acquitted and set free.

MANTLE or CLOAK.—Be warned of treachery on the part of someone whom you trust.

MANUFACTORY.—This dream is very similar in meaning to **MACHINERY.** It relates entirely to commercial prosperity.

MANURE.—To dream that you are cultivating the soil is a good sign for those in subordinate situations, but it is not so fortunate for the wealthy.

MAP.—To dream that you are studying a Map indicates a change of residence, probably also of business or employment. If the Map is coloured, the omen is a fortunate one.

MARBLE.—This is really a luxury dream, and indicates disappointment and loss.

MARCHING.—To dream of Marching quickly predicts advancement and success in business.

MARIGOLDS.—See under **COLOUR.** Most flowers owe their power in a dream to their colour. But as a rule, they are fortunate, and will to some extent counteract any bad influences at work against you.

MARINER or SAILOR.—To dream that you are a Sailor is a sign of restlessness and change in your affairs. But to dream that you are in the company of Sailors shows news from a distance, the arrival of some friend.

MARKET.—To dream that you are in a Market, doing business or buying goods, is a fortunate sign and shows that your circumstances will be comfortable. But if you are idly looking on, then it is a warning of lost opportunities. If the Market is empty or unattended, then expect difficulties and troubles.

MARMALADE or JAM.—To dream that you are eating Preserves by yourself is a bad sign, though it does not foretell great trouble or worry. To enjoy it with others is a fortunate omen. To dream that you are making Jam or Marmalade is good for your love affairs.

MARRIAGE or MARRYING.—To dream that you witness a Marriage is a warning of ill-health. But if you assist at the ceremony, it shows some pleasing news, not of great importance. To dream that you are being Married, either as Bride or Bridegroom, is a most unfortunate omen.

MARSH or BOG.—This is another obstacle dream, and its meaning depends upon what happens to you—trouble and difficulties if you find it hard to move along; but if you get out all right on to firm ground, then you will be able to put right most of the misfortune.

MASK.—To dream that someone comes to you wearing a Mask or a disguise, is a sure sign of treachery.

MASCOTS.—Unexpected news will change your future prospects. Be on guard against a woman's enmity.

MASON.—To dream that you are building a house, or employ someone to do so for you, is a sign of loss due to illness. It is a very unfortunate dream.

MAST.—To dream of the Mast of a ship is considered to be a sign of a coming journey of importance.

MASTER.—If you dream of your employer, it is a favourable omen for your prosperity.

MASTIFF or DOG.—Beware of false suspicions if you see a big Dog in your dream. If he bites you, it is a warning of trouble in your love affairs. But if a woman dreams of a Mastiff, it is a sign that her lover is faithful to her.

MASS.—To dream of attending Mass is a good sign for your future well-being.

MAT.—To dream of a Mat, either in a room or at the door, is held to indicate trouble.

MATCHES.—Financial gains are at hand.

MATTRESS.—A warning of poverty ahead; guard against it.

MAY.—An unfortunate dream; disappointment and bad news are indicated.

MAYPOLE.—Joy and happiness. Sign of festivities.

MAZE.—Should you find your way out in your dream, your perplexities will be happily solved. If you are unable to get out, beware of being dominated by insincere friends.

MEADOW or FIELD.—This is a fortunate dream in every way, for business man or lover. There may, however, be obstacles or difficulties suggested, such as gates, stiles, walls, or possibly a bull.

MEAL.—Poverty, if you are making a good Meal. The opposite if there is little to eat.

MEASURING.—A warning not to carry carefulness to the point of stinginess or you may lose more than you save.

MEASLES.—See ILLNESS, ACHE, DISEASE.

MEAT.—It is not considered fortunate to eat Meat in your dream; though it is all right if you cook it for other people.

MEDALS.—To dream of wearing them, merry times are to come soon.

MEDITERRANEAN SEA.—To visit towns on the shores of this Sea, indicates prosperity in the future.

MEDLARS.—Your enjoyment will cease and trouble ensue.

MEDICINE.—To dream that you are taking Medicine is a warning that your troubles are not serious; persevere and you will succeed.

MELANCHOLY.—A dream of contrary. All will go well.

MELODY.—All pleasant music is a fortunate omen. Persevere and success will attend you.

MELONS.—See **FRUIT.**

MEMORY.—Loss of Memory in a dream presages a rise in the world shortly.

MENAGERIE.—Wild animals in confinement are not a good omen. You may expect difficulties in your business affairs.

MENDING.—To dream of darning clothes portends an inferior and miserable position.

MENDICANT or BEGGAR.—This is a dream of contrary meaning. If you dream that you are reduced to Begging in the streets, it shows that your affairs are prospering. To dream that you are accosted in the street by a Beggar is a sign of difficulty ahead; if you assist the person, you will overcome your trouble by means of a good friend who will help you.

MERMAID.—An unlucky dream, particularly for those in whose lives the ocean plays an important part—seamen, fishermen, etc.

MERRIMENT.—All excessive enjoyment in a dream is a bad omen. Expect difficulties in your home life.

MESMERISM.—To dream you are Mesmerised is a sign of betrayed confidences. Make none and you need not fear.

MESSAGE.—To dream a Message is given you means a change to a better position.

METALS.—See **IRON, LEAD.** To dream of Gold indicates trouble ahead, but there will be no immediate change. You will have time to put things right. To dream of Silver, indicates a disappointment in love that will not prove as unpleasant as you anticipate. To dream of Copper coins is an indication of small but vexatious worries.

MICROSCOPE.—Increase of family.

MICE.—An indication of trouble through a friend or a business associate.

MIDWIFE.—This portends news of a birth; also the discovery of a secret.

MIGNONETTE.—This fragrant blossom is a very favourable omen. Great happiness is coming to you.

MILDEW.—An introduction to an attractive stranger in your own home. Be careful of your private papers.

MILESTONE.—Avoid borrowing if in difficulties. Take no notice of information made known through eaves-dropping.

MIRAGE.—To dream of a Mirage in the desert signifies the loss of the one friend in whom you have trusted.

MILK.—To dream that you are drinking Milk is a fortunate sign; but it is unfortunate if you sell Milk in your dream. To give Milk to some other person is a good omen for those in love. It is also a very good sign to dream that you are Milking a cow, provided the animal is docile and quiet.

MILK-PAILS.—To dream of carrying full Milk-pails is a sign of good news concerning a birth.

MILLET.—Much happiness.

MILLS.—See **MANUFACTORY.**

MILLSTONE.—Increase of family.

MINES.—Your business will increase.

MINT.—To the sick, recovery; to those in good health, better spirits.

MINCE PIES.—Closely connected with Christmas festivities, it is considered good fortune to dream of Mince Pies at any other time of year—not when they are naturally in your thoughts.

MINISTER.—It is not a good sign to see a Clergyman in your dreams. Expect a serious disappointment.

MIRROR.—See **LOOKING-GLASS.**

MIRE.—This signifies anxiety and strife, but should you get out of the muddy place in your dream, your worries will soon pass.

MIRACLE.—Unexpected events will astonish and occupy you for some little while.

MISER.—An unfavourable dream, for the more you hoard, the more unfortunate you will prove in business. It is a bad sign, particularly for those in love.

MISFORTUNE.—This is a dream of contrary. If you dream that some Misfortune happens to yourself or to someone you love, it shows some fortunate stroke of business that will result in a far greater success than you expect.

MISTLETOE.—Take no chances of any kind. You are not in favour with Fortune.

MISSIONARY.—A change to more interesting work and to truer friends. Do not be made unhappy by the desertion of a fickle companion.

MIST.—A warning of difficulties which will beset your path owing to bad trade conditions.

MISTAKE.—Avoid conceit and make sure of your information before acting. Take counsel of those who are willing to guide you.

MOANS.—Be on your guard against doubtful friends, or dubious actions.

MOCKING.—Take care not to be swindled. You will be asked to assist others. Do not neglect your own affairs while trying to settle those of others.

MOLLUSC.—Mysterious happenings will claim your attention. There is usually an explanation of the uncanny. Do not believe, too easily, all you hear.

MONASTERY.—Worldly affairs will prosper.

MOLE.—You will come to grief.

MONARCH.—To dream of your sovereign ruler is a sign of difficulties which can be overcome by hard work. Keep at it, and all will go well.

MONEY.—To dream that you pay or give Money to other people is a fortunate omen ; prosperity awaits you. To dream that you receive Money also foretells personal success, but due to hard work. To find Money in your dream is not so fortunate, however—there will be some sudden advancement or success, but it will prove disappointing. If you change Money, it is a sign of difficulties due to your own fault—as if you exchange notes for silver, or silver for copper. It is a very bad sign if you dream that you borrow Money, either from a friend or from a moneylender.

MONK.—As with others connected with the Church, this is an omen of disappointment and trouble.

MONKEY.—See **APE.**

MONSTER.—To see a Monster in the sea is not good; but out of the sea, good luck.

MONUMENT.—Any handsome Monument is a good omen. Success is coming your way, as a reward of effort.

MOON.—This dream depends upon the circumstances. If the Moon is bright and shines clearly, free from cloud, it foretells success in love, personal happiness. If the Moon is clouded over, it shows ill-health, or some other interruption to your comfort and enjoyment. A New Moon is fortunate for business; a Full Moon for love affairs. See also **COMET.**

MOONSHINE.—Happiness in wedded life. A devoted family.

MOOR.—To walk over Moorlands signifies prosperity, especially should the way lie uphill.

MOP.—You will need forethought and carefulness to avoid coming trouble.

MORNING.—An excellent sign. Your fate is protected from evil. Be confident.

MOSS.—Take care of your correspondence. Write guardedly; seal and post carefully. Someone has an attraction towards you which will soon be expressed.

MOTH or BUTTERFLY.—A warning of rivals who will harm you if you are not careful in your speech and actions. Expect quarrels with your lover, husband, or wife. To those who employ others it is a sign that they are not being served faithfully.

MOTHER.—To dream that you see your Mother and converse with her is a very favourable omen. See also **FATHER.**

MOTH-EATEN CLOTHES.—Someone near to you is in trouble of which you will soon hear, but may not be able to assist.

MOTHER-OF-PEARL.—Your happiest times lie in the future.

MOTOR-CAR.—If you are riding in one, new surroundings are portended.

MOULDY.—Financial gains are coming your way. Do not speculate or you may not keep them long.

MOULTING.—You would be wise to cut doubtful associations and make fresh ties. A small invitation will give you the opportunity to make worth-while friendships.

MOUNTAIN.—Another dream indicating obstacles in your path—the ultimate result depends upon the circumstance. If you climb to the top, all will go well, though it means hard work, as unexpected difficulties will confront you.

MOURNING.—A dream of contrary; as also is **FEASTING** and jollification. Great prosperity is before you, if you are a business man, or married happiness if you are a lover.

MOUSTACHE.—Small disagreements. Do not let them deepen into trouble.

MOUTH.—To dream of your own Mouth means a hint to guard your tongue. To see a small Mouth signifies money to come; a large one, a companion worth more than money.

MOVIES.—Frivolous invitations. Do not trust fair women.

MOVING or REMOVAL.—It is not a fortunate dream to see your furniture being Removed from one house to another It represents an obstacle. If you see everything settled in comfort before the dream ends, then all will be well.

MOWING.—To dream that you are cutting the grass on your lawn shows success in business.

MUD.—A dream of contrary. Good fortune awaits you.

MUDDLE.—Look to your footing, especially in high places. Take no risks of a fall. Pleasure from a re-established friendship.

MUFF.—To dream of this old-fashioned article is a warning of unfaithfulness on the part of someone whom you trust.

MULBERRIES.—This fruit shows a fortunate journey, or a prosperous marriage.

MULTIPLYING.—Do not trust acquaintances till time has proved them.

MUMMY.—Be confident. Success is not far off.

MURDER.—See **MANSLAUGHTER.** Naturally this dream is even more serious in its warning than Man-slaughter, for it shows that you have lost control of your difficulties. You cannot expect to succeed, so should do your utmost to lessen your liabilities and your risks.

MUSHROOMS.—If you see yourself gathering Mush-rooms, your ventures will be fortunate. But if you are eating them, then be cautious in your business affairs.

MUSIC.—To dream that you hear pleasant Music is a very favourable dream ; all your affairs will prosper. It often indicates pleasant news from an absent friend, or the renewal of some old friendship. But harsh and un-pleasant Music is a warning, especially to lovers or married people, for it shows some cunning and underhand action that will cause you great discomfort or loss.

MUSICIAN.—If you dream that you are a Musician, when this is not the case, it is supposed to show a sudden change in your life. Probably you will move to another district. If you really are a Musician, amateur or professional, then the dream is of no importance.

MUTTON.—See **BEEF.**

MYSTERY.—To dream of some happening that puzzles and disturbs you is really an obstacle dream. Solve the mystery, and all will be well.

MUSTARD.—Danger from free speech. Try to avoid hearing or repeating confidences.

MUSIC-HALL.—A good omen for your later life. Your circumstances will improve.

MUTINY.—Your undertakings will lead you into odd company. Keep your promises, but avoid making rash ones.

MYSTIC.—To dream of this is a sign that your mind is set on worldly matters. Allow your interest to broaden if you would be happy.

MYRTLE.—A love avowal.

N

NAGGING.—To dream of being Nagged signifies that you will be the recipient of pleasing information. Be careful in whom you confide it.

NAILS.—It is a very good omen when you find your Nails grown long in your dream ; it denotes prosperity in business, success in love.

NAKED.—It is most fortunate to dream that you are Naked or only very partially clad. Any troubles will be of your own making, and you will not find it easy to get anyone to help you in your difficulties. It is particularly fortunate for lovers, as it shows reliability. To married people, it foretells great happiness.

NAME.—If someone calls you by the wrong Name in a dream, it is an unfortunate omen for your love affairs.

NAPKIN.—Some pleasant news is coming to you soon.

NARCISSUS.—A happy future is certain for those who dream of these beautiful early flowers. But the luck will be lessened if you dream that they are indoors, in pots, or cut and in a bowl. For the best result they should be growing in a garden.

NARROW.—Struggling along a Narrow path in a dream means that every effort will be required to lead you to success, but that you will attain it when almost despairing.

NAVAL BATTLE.—Promotion in the Service for a great friend or relative.

NAVIGATING A VESSEL.—A long journey.

NAVY.—Dreams of the Navy foretell love troubles.

NECK.—To dream that your Neck is troubling you, or that you are worrying over it, is a sign that money is coming to you before long.

NECKLACE.—To dream that you are wearing jewellery around your neck is a very fortunate omen. See **NECK**. But it favours your love affairs more than your business ventures. But if the Necklace breaks or falls from the Neck, then there will be quarrels and disappointments in married life.

NEEDLES or PINS.—Disappointments in love; it will be very serious if you prick yourself.

NEEDLEWORK.—To dream of Needlework is a sign of treachery on the part of someone whom you trust.

NEGATIVES.—Photographic Negatives are good omens of your ability to foresee and avert danger. You will need your powers.

NEGRO.—It is a sign of quarrels with your friends if you dream of any foreign person.

NEIGHING.—It is an unfortunate omen to dream of the Neighing of a horse.

NEIGHBOURS.—To dream of your Neighbours is an omen of coming misfortune or business loss.

NERVOUSNESS.—The solution of a puzzle will occur to you after long thought and bring you great good luck.

NEST OF BIRD.—One of Nature's most fortunate omens. Prosperity and honour are certain to come your way, unless the eggs are broken, or the Nest contains dead youngsters.

NETTLES.—This dream depends upon whether you sting

yourself, for that is a bad sign. Some friend or your sweetheart will deceive you, and cause you much trouble by their lies. But Nettles and Weeds by themselves are a dream of contrary, and show good fortune is ahead of you.

NET-BALL.—Do not be upset by disappointing correspondence ; your success is assured in the end.

NETS.—Omens of prosperous times to come.

NEWS.—It is not a good omen to hear news in your dream, unless it is painful or worrying—in fact, it is a dream of contrary.

NEWSPAPERS.—If in your dream you are reading a Newspaper, it is a sign that a fortunate change will come in your circumstances, but from a distant source.

NEW YEAR.—An improvement in circumstances is at hand. You have an unscrupulous rival ; be careful of your confidences.

NIB.—Not a good sign ; if you dream of breaking it, misfortune is portended.

NIBBLING.—Be careful what you write or sign and you will find that all your good times are to come.

NICK-NACK.—See under **KNICK-KNACK**, an alternative spelling.

NICKNAME.—It is a good omen to hear people call you by a familiar Nickname in your dream.

NIGHT or DARKNESS.—To dream that you are suddenly overtaken by Night, or by an unexplained Darkness is a bad sign ; misfortune will be your lot. But if you persevere, in your dream, and once more see the light of day, then you will recover your losses.

NIECE.—Mutual affection and assistance between you and a relation.

NIGHT-BIRDS.—To dream of Owls, or Bats, or any creatures associated only with Darkness, is a bad sign. See **NIGHT.** But in this case the trouble will not last long.

NIGHTCAP.—An unexpected kiss will cause much jealousy ; beware of practical jokes.

NIGHTSHADE.—To dream you eat the fruits of this deadly plant is a favourable dream, meaning new interests and surroundings.

NIGHT-WALKS.—To dream of walking in the Night signifies trouble.

NIGHTINGALE.—To listen to any sweet-singing Bird in your dream is a fortunate sign ; Nature is favourable. It is also an omen of restored health to an invalid.

NIGHTMARE.—To imagine that you are Dreaming, or have Nightmare, in your dream, is a warning to you of treachery on the part of someone you trust.

NINEPINS or SKITTLES.—To dream that you are playing Skittles is a sign that your affairs are unsettled ; you will experience many ups and downs in the next few weeks. There may be a disappointment in love.

NOISE.—To hear a loud Noise in your dream is a sign of quarrels among your friends or relatives. The louder the Noise, the more serious the result.

NOSE.—To dream that you are bleeding at the Nose is an omen of failing business—be careful in your investments and speculations. It often shows trouble in your home circle. Do not travel, for it will not be fortunate for you, and avoid lending money for the next few weeks.

NOBILITY.—It is a bad omen to dream that you are mixing socially with people of superior standing.

NOSEGAY.—To dream of Flowers is usually very fortunate, but they should be given to you, or appear ready cut in your dream. It is a bad sign to pluck Flowers, for your hopes will be as short-lived as the blossoms.

NOVEL.—All printed matter is unfortunate in your dreams. Be careful of your business affairs and speculations.

NUMBNESS.—To dream that you feel Numb is generally a matter of physical health ; it is not an omen in itself. Consult a doctor.

NODDING.—A warning not to overtry your strength. Danger of illness is around you.

NOOSE.—Obstacles and competition, with which you must hold your own.

NORTH.—To dream of a journey towards the North or of being in Northern places signifies an uphill struggle for you which will end in a great success.

NOSE-BLEED.—Not a good sign. Take the utmost care of yourself for a time.

NUGGET.—An excellent omen of riches and honour.

NUISANCE.—Disagreeable news and unhappiness.

NUMBERS.—To count the Number of persons present in your dream foretells power, satisfied ambition, and dignity. Luck numbers : 3, 7, 9, 11 and 17.

NUN.—These Sisters of Mercy are always associated with Black, which is not a fortunate omen in a dream. Be careful of the motives of the people around you, for you are liable to be deceived.

NURSE.—It is a good sign to dream of a Nurse, and your business affairs will prosper.

NURSERY.—As with Babies, it is not considered a good omen to dream that you are in a Nursery.

NURSING.—It is a favourable omen to dream that you are Nursing someone, especially if the patient is progressing favourably in your care.

NUTS.—As a rule, it is a fortunate dream that includes Nuts, whether they appear as dessert, or are seen on a tree. But they refer to the family fortunes, rather than to your business affairs generally. Some important wish will be gratified.

NUTMEGS.—A probable change in your business will lead to travel overland.

NUTSHELLS.—You will rise to an influential position. If you should dream of stepping on and smashing them, the omen is even luckier.

NUT-TREES.—Dreaming that you see Nut-trees and that you crack and eat their fruit, signifies riches and content gained with labour and pain.

O

OAK TREE.—Any dream that includes a flourishing Tree may be looked upon as a fortunate omen—the finer the Tree, the better the immediate prospects. If, however, you see healthy young Trees, it is still a good sign, but you will not benefit fully for some years. If the Tree is withered, or if the leaves have fallen, it is a warning of business losses ; while if the Tree has been felled, and is lying in your path, it is a very serious omen.

OAR.—It is a good omen if you dream of rowing in a small boat. If others are also rowing with you, then expect to face difficulties before success, It is a bad sign if you lose or break an Oar.

OATS or CORN.—Success in commerce follows a dream of a growing crop, whether it is Corn, Oats, or Barley. If the crop is still green or unripe, be careful for a few months, or you may make a serious blunder. See also **CORN-FIELD.**

OBLIGATION.—It is not a good sign to dream that you are under an Obligation to someone, or that someone is doing you a good turn.

OCEAN or SEA.—This dream depends entirely upon circumstances. If the water is quiet and peaceful, it is a good sign, whether it is the Sea, or a lake or a river. But if it is stormy or rough, then beware, for you have a difficult time before you, and will need all your courage.

OASIS.—To dream of wandering in a desert and finding an Oasis is a sign of one friend on whose help you can always rely.

OATH.—A comfortable salary and good position will be yours.

OBELISK.—You will move from your present surroundings and meet with better luck and new friends elsewhere.

OBEYING.—You have an admirer who is seriously attracted. Do not be depressed by sad tidings from a distance, brighter days are in store.

OBITUARY.—To read of the death of someone you know well means news of their marriage.

OBSERVATORY.—A solitary life will be your fate if you reject your friends as you are doing.

OCCUPATION.—To dream of doing work you detest means good fortune in every way.

OCULIST.—You are being watched ; do not be ensnared.

ODOURS.—Fragrant scents signify contentment ; unpleasant odours mean vexation.

OFFENCE.—To dream that some person has Offended you, is a warning of family quarrels that will affect your position or your domestic comfort. If you have given cause for Offence, then the fault will certainly lie at your own door.

OFFER.—It is considered fortunate if someone makes a good Offer for your services in your dream. Expect an improvement in your position, but you must work hard.

OFFICE.—To dream that you have lost your situation, or that your landlord has turned you out of your Office, is a warning of trouble in your love affairs, or married life.

OFFICER.—Guard your speech and letters alike. Important happenings will claim your attention.

OGRE.—To dream of imaginary Monsters is not a good sign. Difficulties and obstacles will come between you and your dearest wish.

OIL.—To dream that you are using Oil in any way is an unfortunate omen, except for women, or those who use it normally, such as artists, painters, or contractors, and so on.

OINTMENT.—A slight illness to come.

OLD.—To dream that you are very Old signifies fame; of Old clothes, you should take courage and think more highly of yourself.

OLD MAN.—For a woman to dream that she is being courted by an Old Man is a fortunate omen; her lover will prove faithful and all that she can desire.

OLD WOMAN.—For a man to dream that he is courting, or married to an Old Woman is a very fortunate omen for his business enterprises. All will go well. To see Old people, without any question of loving them, is fortunate, but in a small and trifling manner. Some unimportant wish will be gratified.

OLD-FASHIONED.—To dream of wearing Old-fashioned clothes signifies dissension in your home life. Be firm, but not angry.

OLD SWEETHEART.—This presages a return to familiar occupations and surroundings; sometimes a proposal is on its way from someone you knew long ago.

OLIVES.—An omen of peace and happiness in domestic life.

OMNIBUS.—This is considered a fortunate omen if you alone are riding in the bus. Every extra passenger represents an obstacle to your success, some difficulty to be overcome.

ONIONS.—A very mixed dream. You will encounter some unexpected good fortune, but it will prove disappointing to you in the end.

OPAL.—This curious gem is considered most favourable when concerned in a dream, in spite of the fact that many people are superstitious and will not wear them in real life.

OPERA.—See **MUSIC.** But success may not be easy to obtain.

OPERATION.—It is an obstacle dream if you imagine that you are undergoing an Operation. Success will come to you if no trouble comes in the dream. It is, however, considered a sign of unexpected news if you watch an Operation performed on someone else. Neither of these meanings would apply in the case of a nurse or a medical man.

OPIUM.—Worries, bad news from the sea or serious illness of someone dear to you is portended by this dream.

OPPONENT.—See **ADVERSARY.**

ORANGE.—See **FRUIT,** and **COLOUR.**

OPTICIAN.—To dream of buying Spectacles means that you have not seen a good chance until it has gone by.

ORATORY.—To dream of listening to an Orator signifies a scolding.

ORANGE BLOSSOM.—This can only mean that your thoughts are concerned with a wedding.

ORCHARD.—To dream that you are in an Orchard is always a favourable sign, but the actual extent of your good fortune will depend on the condition of the fruit. If it is ripe and plentiful, you may expect great success ; if it is green or scarce, then your fortunes will mend, but it will require time and patience.

ORCHESTRA.—Music is generally considered a fortunate omen in a dream, but in the case of an Orchestra, there will be too many difficulties and failure generally results.

ORDERS.—To dream of wearing them, a setback to your hopes.

ORGAN.—This is a fortunate dream, unless the music is too loud to be pleasant to you personally, or if a funeral march is being played. It is very favourable for love affairs.

ORIENT.—To dream of Oriental people or countries is an omen of romantic happiness which will not prove lasting. Do not be too absorbed in it.

ORPHANS.—Whoever dreams of Orphans will receive profits or riches by the hand of a stranger.

ORNAMENTS.—A dream of contrary. The more Ornaments you wear in your dream, the greater will be the coming trouble.

OSTLER.—To dream of Stablemen or anything to do

with horses is a good omen. You are in favour with Fortune and will have luck in all undertakings.

OSTRICH.—A slight ailment will worry you ; look to your diet.

OTTER.—False friends will hurt your feelings, but not your fortunes.

OTTOMAN or COUCH.—This is not considered a good omen for love affairs, or domestic life.

OVEN.—To dream that you are baking or cooking some food in an Oven is a sign that your affairs have reached a standstill. If you burn the food, you will drift slowly to the bad ; if the result is a pleasant meal, then in time you will prosper. But in any case you should be very careful for some time, and certainly take no risks.

OVERALLS.—To dream of working in an Overall, you will be well repaid for a small kindness. To tear it, means ill-luck.

OVERBOARD.—To dream that you have fallen into the water from some boat or vessel is a sign of misfortune. Do not speculate, or you will lose your money. But to the sailor or anyone professionally connected with the water, this becomes a dream of contrary, and foretells prosperity.

OVERCOAT.—The more clothes you wear, the greater the coming trouble.

OVERFLOWING.—An excellent omen of financial success.

OVERTAKING.—This means advancement in position and the good influence of one whom you have known on or by the sea.

OVERWORK.—A difference in your life either in your feelings or your business.

OVERTURNED.—If a woman dreams she be Overturned while riding, it is a sign that she shall be greatly distressed for a short time. For a man to have this dream denotes that some animal to which he is attached will sicken and perhaps die.

OXEN.—To dream that you see a herd of Oxen is a very fortunate sign ; your affairs will prosper. If they are grazing peacefully, your speculations or investments should be watched, as they should show signs of favourable development. Buy and sell shares carefully. See **COW.**

OYSTERS.—To dream of eating Oysters is a sign that you have hard work in front of you, and that you will need courage if you are to succeed. But in love affairs, it promises happiness if you are patient.

P

PACK.—It is an omen of contrary to dream that you are Packing for a journey—business worries will keep you at home.

PACKET.—A disappointment is in front of you—work hard or you will have to face trouble. The bigger the Packet that comes to you, the greater the trouble. It is a good sign if you open the Packet.

PADLOCK.—This is an obstacle dream. Note carefully whether the Padlock fastens you in, or whether you use it to fasten some door.

PADDOCK.—Do not speculate or you will most likely lose ; news of an engagement will surprise you.

PAGEANT.—A warning against judging by appearances or paying too much attention to outward things.

PAGODA.—A journey will be cancelled through sudden news.

PAIL.—An unfortunate omen ; be careful of your new business ventures.

PAIN.—A dream of contrary. The greater your suffering in your dream, the more successful you will be in real life. To lovers, it is extremely fortunate. See **ACHE** and **ILLNESS.**

PAINT.—See **OIL.**

PAINTER.—Good fortune.

PAINTING.—Domestic affliction.

PALACE.—It is a good sign, for those in lowly circumstances, to dream of Palaces or showy houses and big estates. It is also favourable for love affairs.

PALL.—Probably a legacy and great sadness through bereavement.

PALLID.—To dream of seeing the face of anyone you know very pale presages danger, perhaps death, to that person.

PALM TREES.—Successful speculations and flourishing business ventures. Some unexpected difficulty will be overcome.

PANCAKE.—To dream that you are eating Pancakes shows some unexpected success ; you will see your way out of some difficulty, perhaps by the assistance of some friend or business associate. But if you are cooking Pancakes, and they break or burn, then your venture will certainly fail.

PANSY.—This pleasant and popular flower is an omen of contentment. There are no big changes for you, but you will be happy.

PANTRY.—To dream that you are in the Pantry is not a good omen. You will succeed up to a certain point, but will always have obstacles to overcome.

PAPER.—To dream of Paper is a sign of some coming trouble. If the Paper is clean, you will escape with a slight money loss. But if the Paper is soiled and dirty, then your own questionable action will prove your undoing. If the Paper is folded, it denotes some small disappointment. See **NEWSPAPER.**

PAPERING A ROOM.—This foretells the illness of a friend.

PARACHUTE.—Be careful of all extremes and do not overwork or overplay.

PARADE.—To see a Parade of soldiers drilling means

that you will quarrel with someone in uniform through hasty words.

PARADISE.—Happy marriage. To the farmer, abundant crops. A good omen to all.

PARALYSIS.—If you dream that you are Paralysed, it is a sign of a broken engagement.

PARAPET.—Dangers and worries which you will surmount by your own efforts.

PARASOL.—It is considered fortunate if you see yourself with your Parasol open—in other words, it is an indirect indication of favourable weather and sunshine.

PARCEL.—To dream that you receive a Parcel is a very fortunate omen; but if you open it, you may affect your luck. If you are carrying a Parcel, expect a change of circumstances.

PARCHED.—A voyage to a hot country is portended.

PARCHMENT.—Legal affairs will trouble you.

PARK.—This dream of a fine open space is a favourable one. See such omens as **PALACE, LANDSCAPE.** If you are accompanied by one other person, it shows a happy love affair; but if several people are with you, then expect difficulties for a time.

PARENT.—See **FATHER** and **MOTHER.**

PARLIAMENT.—To dream that you are a Member of Parliament, means advancement; if you are a visitor, quarrels.

PARROT.—Hard work is before you; you will suffer from the idle talk of other people.

PARSLEY.—Like most green things, this is an omen of success that has been achieved by hard work.

PARSNIP.—Subjection to a master is denoted.

PARTRIDGE or GAME.—Many small troubles and worries. If the Birds fly away, you will succeed in the end, but it will need courage and patience.

PARTY.—It is considered a fortunate omen to dream that you are at a Party, but it is unfavourable if you yourself give a Party, and the smarter the function the worse the omen.

PASSAGE.—This is really an obstacle dream. The longer the Passage, the greater the difficulties you will overcome.

PASSION or TEMPER.—It is a warning of trouble, generally domestic, to lose your Temper in a dream.

PASTRY.—See **PANCAKE.** This is a very similar dream, and is a warning that you should move carefully, both in business and in love affairs.

PASTE.—To dream of imitation jewellery is a sign of inferior friends.

PASSION FLOWER.—To dream of this flower signifies sacrifice and sorrow.

PASTING.—Loss of a friend, but success to your plans.

PATCHWORK.—An excellent dream ; money will come to you in an unexpected way.

PATCH.—To dream of a Patch on your garments betokens inherited wealth.

PATTERN.—Small vexations of home life are indicated, but your greater worries will be overcome.

PATH.—This is another obstacle dream, as the meaning depends upon circumstances. If you can walk easily and comfortably, then your affairs will flourish. If you meet stiles or other obstacles to your progress, then you may be certain that there are difficulties to be faced in the future.

PAWNBROKER or PAWNING.—This dream certainly foretells heavy losses and disappointments. Your sweetheart will prove unfaithful ; or if you are married, some indiscreet action of your partner will cause great trouble.

PAY.—It is not fortunate to see yourself Paying away money in a dream, even if you are settling a debt.

PEACH.—See **FRUIT**, also **COLOUR.** A dream of personal pleasure, not of business affairs.

PEACOCK.—A dream of contrary—your fine plans will fail, and you will be disappointed. But to the farmer, this handsome bird foretells a good harvest, after much hard work.

PEARLS.—A very favourable dream, but you will have to earn your success by hard work. Be patient, for you will surely succeed. If Pearls are given to you in your dream, it is a sign of a very happy and successful marriage. If the string of Pearls should break, however, it shows grief and sorrow, unless you thread them again in your dream.

PEARS.—See **FRUIT.**

PEAS.—This is a fortunate dream on the whole, but you must exercise patience, particularly if the Peas are raw, or not cooked sufficiently. It is most favourable when you see the Peas growing in the garden. Dried Peas show money, but acquired in a doubtful manner.

PEASANT.—For a townsman to dream of a Peasant is a good sign of business plans which will prosper.

PEBBLES.—Jealousy and competition will trouble you.

PEDESTRIAN or WALKER.—It is generally far more fortunate in a dream to be walking, instead of riding.

PEDLAR.—To dream of a Pedlar signifies deceitful companions.

PENANCE.—Be reserved with strangers; a dangerous influence is near you when travelling.

PENCIL.—Take note of the friend who gave it to you in the dream, as a parting from that person is indicated.

PENDULUM.—A sudden message will cause you to take a long journey.

PEONY.—Not a good flower to dream about; it denotes anxiety and annoyance.

PENS.—News about absent friends.

PENSION.—You will be called upon to make a decision. Be careful to decide as you really wish.

PEPPER.—Talent in your family, particularly if you sniff the Pepper till you sneeze.

PEPPERMINT. You will be proud of your offspring's attainments, if not your own.

PERAMBULATOR.—Responsibilities will hamper you.

PERCH.—A higher position is in store for you if you

dream of climbing to a bough or tree-top. Do not let it alter your friendships.

PERFORM.—To dream of Performing signifies too great an attachment to appearances.

PERFUME or SCENT.—This is always a favourable dream, both for the man of commerce or the lover.

PERIL.—It is an obstacle omen if you find yourself in Peril in your dream. If you come off successfully, then all will go well.

PERJURY or TELLING LIES.—A bad dream, for you will deserve the misfortune that will befall you.

PERSIAN.—To dream of Eastern materials signifies an addiction to laziness which would not be for your good if you were able to indulge it.

PERSPIRATION.—Great efforts will be required of you and duly rewarded.

PEST.—To dream of house or garden Pests is a token of prosperity beyond your hopes.

PETROL.—Danger of fires and disputes; guard against either.

PETTICOAT.—A dream of warning against conceit and dissipation; keep to moderate ways and feelings.

PEWTER.—Contentment and joy but not wealth.

PHANTOM or GHOST.—Disappointment in store for you. For lovers, a Ghost dream shows a successful rival, or the fickleness of the one you love. Be careful to avoid quarrels with your friends, or fate is against you. Do not travel, and avoid lending money or giving extra credit in business.

PHEASANT.—See **PARTRIDGE.**

PHOTO.—It is always fortunate to look at a Photo of some other person in a dream, but not at your own. It is a bad omen to have your Photograph taken.

PHYSICIAN or DOCTOR.—This is a very fortunate omen—It is always a good sign to see or speak to a Doctor in your dream.

PIANO.—See **FIDDLES, MUSIC.**

PICK UP.—See **GATHER.**

PICNIC.—A doubtful sign concerning your love affairs. The meaning depends upon what happens at the Picnic.

PICTURES.—To dream of Pictures is a bad omen, for it warns you of treachery by one you trust. The more pleasing the Pictures appear to you, the more dangerous the omen. It means work without profit.

PICTURE PALACE.—A good omen of general well-being to come.

PIE.—To dream of cooking one means homely joys; to eat one, dissension in the family.

PIER.—You will see another's happiness, but your own will follow some day.

PIGS.—A very mixed dream, for good and bad luck will both be present in your affairs. Many of your cherished plans will fail, yet others, apparently less important, will succeed and restore the balance. Watch over the members of your household, as trouble may reach you from this source.

PIGEONS.—News of importance from afar, but it may not be very favourable. It will mean changes in your affairs. They are favourable for love affairs, and is it better to see them flying in the air, than walking on the ground, or settling on ledges.

PILGRIM.—This dream promises the fulfilment of a great wish.

PILLOW.—A clean Pillow is a good sign, but if it is soiled and untidy, then expect troubles of your own making.

PILLS.—A journey abroad with many pleasures at the end of it.

PILOT.—Cheery scenes and good times ahead but you will be defeated by a rival in the end.

PINAFORE.—A great deal of pleasure from a small present; be circumspect in your actions or you will make your position very difficult.

PINE TREE.—This signifies good news of elderly people but danger to the young.

PIN-CUSHION.—It is a favourable sign if there are plenty of Pins stuck in the Cushion. If not, then expect disappointment.

PINE-APPLE.—Comfortable domestic surroundings; invitations and pleasure-seeking. See **FRUIT.**

PINS.—See **NEEDLES.**

PINKS.—These portend gay times and new garments, especially if the dreamer sells them.

PIPE.—A sign of unusual events resulting in good fortune to the smoker.

PIRATE.—Exciting times, journeys and financial gains; the deceit of an associate will cause you pain.

PISTOL.—To hear the sound of firing foretells misfortune. If you yourself fire the Pistol, it is a sign of hard work, with very little result therefrom.

PIT.—This is really an obstacle dream. If you descend into a Pit or deep hollow, it shows that your business affairs will decline. To a lover, it means that he will meet with coldness or indifference. If you *fall* into the Pit, it is a most unfortunate omen, for you will suffer for a long time from troubles confronting you.

PITCH.—An evil omened dream in some ways. You will obtain money easily but your reputation is in danger.

PITY.—To dream of being Pitied means humiliation, of Pitying someone else, small vexations.

POACH.—A very fortunate dream indeed; keep a guard on your speech for a time and everything you undertake will be accomplished.

POETRY (writing).—A present of jewellery soon to be offered you, possibly a ring. If the dreamer is a man he should guard his writings; if a girl, her feelings; if a wife, her fidelity of heart.

POLICE.—This might be called a dream of contrary, for if you dream of trouble with the Police, it shows that some present difficulty will be overcome.

POMEGRANATE.—A happy augury; honours will come to you.

POND or LAKE.—It is a good sign for lovers if the Pond

is quiet and clear-looking. Look out for trouble if the Pond is dirty or full of mud.

POPPIES.—Temptation will come your way. Be on your guard and do not yield.

PLAGUE.—Lucky discovery and wealthy marriage.

PLAID.—A dream signifying health and a kindly companion.

PLAINS.—To journey over Plains signifies material gains but loss of the affection of one you care for.

PLANK.—A sign of a restless state of mind which only travel will satisfy.

PLANTS.—See **HERBS.**

PLASTER.—False accusations will be made against you if you dream that the Plaster is upon you, but if you dream that the Plaster is coming off the walls of your house the trouble is for your family.

PLATFORM.—You will marry where you least expect to ; beware of hasty judgments.

PLAY.—See **THEATRE.**—It is more fortunate to watch a Play than to dream that you are taking part in one.

PLEADING.—Take confidence in your own powers ; their strength and confidence will soon be proved to you and others.

PLEASURE.—Always a dream of contrary. The more boisterous your mirth in your dream, the greater your loss or difficulty will be in your business affairs.

PLOT.—Important correspondence will claim your attention ; changes, surprises and a possible engagement will ensue.

PLOUGH.—It is a good omen to see someone Ploughing a field, though it also indicates hard work. To the lover, it indicates patience, for some time must pass before his affection can be crowned. If you are yourself Ploughing, it shows that your hard work will not appear successful at first ; but you must persevere and you will overcome your troubles. This indicates great happiness in married life to the patient lover.

PLUME.—Unexpected gain and public honour, especially if the Plume be white.

PLUMS.—It is a good dream if you are gathering ripe Plums ; but if they are still green, then your efforts will fail from want of careful planning. If you pick up the fruit after it has fallen to the ground, it is a sign of change of position, not entirely for your good. Dried Plums—such as Prunes—show difficulties.

PLUNDER.—A dangerous mistake ; act with candour about it and avoid angry discussion if you would lessen the trouble.

POISON.—To dream that you have taken Poison is a warning of financial loss through the dishonesty of some person whom you trust. Be careful how you give credit or lend money. Do not speculate or buy shares or stocks. If you recover from the effects of the Poison, you will get over your difficulties if you exercise care and tact.

PORCUPINE.—This unusual creature indicates difficulties in your business affairs.

PORTER.—Slander and annoyance.

PORTRAIT.—A warning of danger regarding the person whose Portrait or Photo is envisioned, especially if it is faded or injured.

POSTMAN.—Some unexpected happening.

POST OFFICE.—A change of residence and companions.

POTATOES.—Do not try to " play Providence " for other people or you may do more harm than good.

POTS.—A sign of coming disappointment. Be careful about your plans and do not talk them over with anyone.

POUCH.—If the dreamer is a man it portends a disclosure much to his advantage.

POUND.—To dream of animals in a Pound signifies a rise in salary and a change of scene.

POULTRY.—A very fortunate dream. See **PIGS**.

POVERTY.—A dream of contrary. Good fortune is coming your way.

POWER.—The higher your position in your dream, the

greater your Power and Authority, the more serious will be the difficulties in your path.

POWDER.—To dream of powdering means a new dress for a festive occasion.

PRAISE.—To dream of being Praised denotes scandal and gossip around you.

PRAYERS.—To dream you offer up Prayers signifies happiness.

PREACHER.—The result of your plans will be satisfactory at last, however worrying at present.

PRECIPICE.—This is another obstacle dream very similar in meaning to **PIT.**—It is a warning of trouble ahead of you, and you should avoid travelling or any change of plans. Take warning and act with prudence. If you fall over the Precipice, it is a bad sign ; but if you walk away from the edge, you will overcome all troubles.

PRESS.—For a woman to dream of putting linen in an old-fashioned Press portends a fine home to be hers before long.

PRESENT.—See **GIFT.**

PRICK.—To dream of a needle Prick to yourself signifies a gift made in a loving spirit.

PRIDE.—You will rise in the world but others will use your promotion for their own ends, especially one whom you trust.

PRIEST.—To dream of a Clergyman is a sign that some quarrel will be cleared up, thus increasing your personal happiness.

PRIMER.—To dream of Lesson-books is a dream of " contraries " and promises a pleasant holiday.

PRINCE OF WALES.—To dream of meeting and speaking with him signifies honours and riches to come ; to see him only a present will be given to you.

PRINT.—To dream of watching the Printing being done signifies success, but be on your guard against dangerous companions.

PRISON.—This is a dream of contrary—see **POLICE.** It indicates much happiness in your home affairs and success in business. To dream that someone is put in Prison through your efforts is not a fortunate sign. You are being too venturesome in your money matters, too eager to secure a profit, and it may mean a loss instead of a gain.

PRIZE.—This is a " contrary " dream foreboding loss through sharp dealing. Be on your guard when offered something cheap.

PROCESSION.—To witness a Procession in your dream is a good sign for the lover or married person. The longer it lasts, the better, for many years of happiness are foretold.

PROMISE.—An important decision for you to make. The right answer will lead to happy times for you, so think well.

PROPOSAL.—If you dream of receiving one, be careful not to be drawn into another person's schemes. Should you make one, exciting times are ahead.

PROMONTORY.—This dream predicts an outstanding event which is just round the corner.

PROPERTY.—This means you will be disappointed in your hopes.

PROVISIONS or FOOD.—To dream that you are hungry and cannot obtain any Food foretells business troubles and loss of money. But it is a fortunate omen to have plenty of Food on your table, or Provisions stored in your larder.

PUBLIC HOUSE.—To dream that you are drinking in a Public House is a bad sign. To lovers, it shows deceit by the person loved and trusted, and much unhappiness. To the farmer it foretells bad crops. To dream that you own a Public House shows that you will have to work hard but that you will eventually recover from your losses and worries.

PUDDING.—A simple meal is a good omen in a dream—it is the banquets and the feasting that foretell trouble.

PULPIT.—Like all omens connected with the interior of a Church, this is not a favourable sign.

PUPPY.—An invitation to a jolly party; laugh with the people you meet there but do not become intimate.

PUMP.—To Pump clear water is a good sign; your business will prosper; if the water is soiled, however, worries and evil speaking will annoy you.

PUNCH.—To dream of drinking it is a warning of unpleasant news to come concerning loss of money and possibly reputation.

PUNISHMENT.—To dream of being Punished signifies an unexpected pleasure at hand.

PURGATORY.—A portent of sickness and travel, but not necessarily to yourself.

PURPLE.—See **COLOUR.**

PURSE.—To dream that you find a Purse is a good omen if money is inside; it is very fortunate for lovers. But if you dream that you have lost your Purse, then expect difficulties or illness, as the result of your own carelessness.

PUSH.—To dream of Pushing against a door or other heavy object signifies that some overmastering obstacle will be removed from your path.

PUTTY.—An omen of hard work and hard times, especially if you dream of using it yourself.

PUZZLE.—An obstacle dream. If you cannot solve the Puzzle, then expect heavy losses in business, for trouble is ahead.

PYRAMIDS.—A successful future and a high position in the world is assured to you.

Q

QUACK.—To dream that you are under the care of Quacks is unfortunate and foretells to the person dreaming that she must beware of these nuisances to society.

QUAILS.—This is an unlucky dream, denoting bad intelligence and family jars. You will lose your lover through false reports.

QUADRUPEDS.—There is no special meaning attached to the sight of four-footed animals in your dream—it all depends upon the animal. But unusual creatures are not considered fortunate omens. Thus a Horse is far better than a Giraffe.

QUAKER.—To dream of these simple and quiet living people is always a fortunate omen.

QUARRELS.—This is one of the dreams of contrary, and foretells prosperity in your business affairs. But there will be opposition for you to face at first. See **DISPUTE.**

QUARRY.—An obstacle dream. If you fall into a Quarry and cannot get out, then expect serious trouble.

QUAY or DOCK.—Shipping is not a fortunate sign as a rule, so it is far better for you if you dream that you view if from a Dock or from the shore.

QUEEN.—See **KING.** A sign of valuable friendships.

QUESTIONS.—To dream that someone is asking you questions is an obstacle omen. If you can answer properly all will go well.

QUILT.—This is a fortunate dream, provided it is properly placed on the bed.

QUEUE.—If you dream of waiting in a Queue, a re-established friendship will lead to marriage.

QUICKSANDS.—This dream denotes that you are surrounded with many temptations. Do not be imprudent.

QUICKSILVER.—You will be invited to an enjoyable festivity. Gossip is on foot concerning you.

QUIVER.—Happiness through the joys of home and marriage.

QUOITS.—To a woman, it denotes some disagreeable and laborious undertaking to go through. To a man, it is a sign of quarrelling.

R

RABBIT.—See **HARE.**

RACE.—One of the ever-recurring obstacle dreams, warning you to persevere if you desire success.

RACECOURSE.—Jolly company but danger of losses through sharp practices.

RACEHORSE.—To see a Racehorse, try to economise while there is time. To ride one, do not speculate, luck is not with you.

RACKET.—This dream betokens loss of leisure which will however be well repaid later by a new friendship.

RADISHES.—Discovery of secrets or domestic jars.

RAFFLE.—This dream of risk and chance is a warning to you that you do not deserve success ; mend your ways and be more generous in your treatment of others. See **LOTTERY.**

RAFT.—To dream of being on one, enforced travel, to see one, a varied life for some time.

RAGE.—See **PASSION.**

RAGS.—This is a fortunate dream. See **NAKED.** Any display in a dream is generally a bad sign.

RAID.—An excellent omen of pleasant times to come.

RAILWAY.—See **LOCOMOTIVE.**

RAIN.—An omen that foretells difficulties in the near future. If the downpour is a heavy one, it becomes a serious warning. See **FOG** and **HAIL.**

RAINBOW.—A fortunate dream, showing that there will certainly be a change in your affairs before long.

RAISINS.—To use them in cooking means several small gifts ; to eat them signifies that you will spend money more easily than you earn it. You must try to economise more.

RAKE.—To Rake hay, a wedding to come ; to Rake leaves, a happy home.

RAM.—Misfortune.

RAMBLE.—A wish will be granted after long delay.

RASH.—A warning against "speaking your mind" before thinking twice as to the result of your words.

RASCAL.—To dream of being duped by a Rascal in business means increased trade and a comfortable income.

RASPBERRY.—See **FRUIT.**

RAT.—An omen of enemies whom you do not suspect. If you see more than One Rat, then the coming trouble will be a serious one, and may overwhelm you. To the lover, it foretells a fortunate rival. White Rats may be sometimes seen ; if so, you will get through your troubles successfully.

RAT-CATCHER.—You can rely on having at least one "friend in need."

RAVEN.—This is really a dream of the colour **BLACK.** Trouble is coming, though you may not deserve it.

RAW.—To dream of Raw food denotes a friend who would like to become a lover.

RAZOR.—Any sharp-cutting instrument is a warning of a coming quarrel. Keep control over yourself.

READING.—It is not a good sign to dream that you are Reading; it foretells a dangerous venture, in which you will probably lose money.

REAPER.—See **CORN** and **HARVEST.**

REAR.—To dream that you are riding a horse that Rears and plunges betokens success in plans that have long seemed impossible to carry out.

REBELLION.—An inferior who has caused you much trouble will soon cease to annoy you.

RECEIPT.—A thrilling time ahead ; be on guard with all but the most trusted friends.

RECITING.—This portends social popularity and a happy marriage.

RECONCILIATION.—This is a favourable sign in a dream. See **PASSION.**

RED.—See **COLOUR.**

REEDS.—Your friends are not all true ; try them well before trusting any.

REEL.—To wind cotton or silk on Reels signifies delayed success achieved by patience.

REFLECTION.—To see your own Reflection in water means a lonely life, but should you dream of a strange face reflected, it is a sign that you will meet and marry the owner.

REFRACTORY.—To dream of Refractory children or animals means that you will be given a highly important post.

REFRESHMENTS.—To offer them, a happy marriage ; to partake of them small vexations.

REFUSAL.—To dream of a Refusal signifies a most certain acceptance.

REGATTA.—A visit to a strange place will bring you fresh work.

REGIMENT.—To see a Regiment of soldiers marching by means serious disputes in which you will be involved shortly.

REGISTRY-OFFICE.—You stand at the cross-roads, decide quickly and do not look back.

REHEARSAL.—To be present at a Rehearsal presages difficulties in the present but honours in the future.

RELEASE.—An ill-omened dream if you should be Released from a prison, but a sign of troubles soon to end if you think you are Releasing someone else.

RELIGION.—It is generally a bad sign to be troubled by Religion in a dream. See **CHURCH** and **CLERGY.**

REMOVAL.—To dream of a Removal means an unexpected visitor to the house.

RENT.—Unexpected gains will be yours following a dream in which you cannot pay Rent or any other debt.

RENT CLOTHES.—To dream of holes in your clothes is a bad sign of losses in your fortune, but should you be mending them in your dream you will soon make good your losses.

REPRIMAND.—This portends an important offer from a superior, which will surprise and delight you.

REPTILE.—See SNAKE.

RESCUE.—To be Rescued is not a good sign, especially from drowning. Avoid travel on sea.

RESERVOIR.—To see one filled with clean water is a good omen of plenty in the future.

RESIGN.—To dream of Resigning your work means advancement in the near future, also money gained through legal matters.

REST.—A "contrary" dream meaning hard work; good luck in sporting matters.

RESTAURANT.—To look on at others eating in a Restaurant signifies ill-health; should you be eating also, small enjoyments amongst new friends.

RESURRECTION.—A long journey to places of religious interest will give you great happiness.

RETURN.—To dream you see someone who has been away for a long time is a sign of losses soon to be made good, and renewed prosperity.

REVELRY.—A "contrary" dream heralding misfortune unless you dream of looking on at the Revelry of others.

REVOLVER.—To dream of handling a Revolver is a sign of danger by water. Try to avoid travelling by sea or river.

REVENGE.—Anxious times, humiliation, and a quarrel, but the latter will soon be made up.

REWARD.—Failure of your plans through over-confidence. Remember there are things money cannot buy.

RHEUMATISM.—To dream of suffering from this signifies a new lease of life and happiness.

RHINOCEROS.—Success in business affairs, but delays and disillusion to those in love.

RHUBARB.—To dream that you handle good Rhubarb is a portent of firm friendship with a late enemy.

RHYMING.—To dream of writing Rhymes betokens worry over business accounts. You are being cheated.

RIB of an UMBRELLA.—To dream your Umbrella has a broken Rib is a very bad sign as to financial matters. Do not be too generous. Gifts are not as important as affection to a true lover.

RIBBON.—A dream of light pleasure and careless spending of money.

RIBS.—To dream of any harm to your body is an unfavourable omen. Look out for treachery among those you trust.

RICE.—Be careful of your plans, for they are ill-advised.

RICHES.—Unfortunately this is a dream of contrary—the more flourishing your affairs in your visionary world, the worse they will be in real life.

RIDDLE.—An unexpected offer from someone related to you. Be on your guard as there is danger in it.

RIDING.—It is a fortunate omen to dream that you are Riding a horse, unless the animal is out of control or throws you.

RINGS.—To lose your Ring is a warning of coming trouble through a friend or relation. It is a fortunate sign if someone makes you a present of a Ring.

RIOT.—This is a warning of financial failure, especially if you see many rioters fighting.

RIVAL.—This should be treated as an obstacle dream ; if you defeat your Rival, or if he retires, you will prove successful in your business affairs.

RIVER.—As with all dreams of water, whether Sea, Lake, or River, the meaning depends upon the clearness or muddiness of the Water. If there are signs of storm, then be very cautious in your plans, for trouble lies ahead. To fall or jump in, shows domestic worries.

RIVET.—To dream of a Rivet, indicates travel by road or rail.

ROAD.—A well-made, broad Road is a most fortunate omen, but lanes or narrow winding paths should be treated as obstacles.

ROAST MEAT.—Affectionate greetings.

ROAR.—The Roar of waters, a traveller will return ; of animals, an enemy is watching you.

ROBBER or THIEF.—It is considered fortunate to be molested by a Thief in your dream, provided you escape injury.

ROBIN.—One of Nature's most fortunate omens.

ROCKET.—Short-lived success is portended. You must build on firmer foundations next time.

ROCKS.—Another obstacle dream, the meaning of which depends upon the circumstances. But it certainly foretells difficulties and hard work.

ROLLS.—New bread signifies promotion in work ; stale Rolls mean tedious business.

ROOF.—Prosperity and festive garments are soon to be yours.

ROOKS.—A journey will be taken by sea or river.

ROOM, A STRANGE.—This unusual dream signifies success after you have almost given up hope. Persevere !

ROOTS.—A difficult task accomplished ; you are letting others get the credit of your ideas. Do not be so weak.

ROPES.—These are obstacle dreams. If you find yourself securely bound with Ropes, then expect a difficult time in your business affairs, for trouble is surely coming.

ROSARY.—To dream that you are telling the beads of your own Rosary means reconciliation with a friend, to see someone wearing a Rosary signifies bereavement.

ROSES.—A most fortunate dream for everybody, unless the blossoms are withered or fall to pieces in your hands. If the flowers are only slightly faded, it foretells success after some difficulties.

ROUGE.—This unnatural trick for " beautifying " yourself artificially is a bad omen. Someone will cheat you, owing to your own carelessness.

ROUSE.—To dream that you Rouse a person from a sleep is good.

RUB.—To dream that you are Rubbing anything denotes marriage and success in business.

ROTTEN.—This signifies the decay of a great family

fortune which will affect you indirectly, whether it be Rotten fruit or timber, but should the dream be of Rotten cliffs which crumble as you climb them, guard your health most carefully.

ROWING.—See **OAR.**

RUBBER.—To erase writing with an india-rubber is a presage of uncertainty of action. Take counsel of older heads than yours.

RUBBISH.—You are about to make a most valuable discovery. Use it, but try not to hurt a friend by doing so.

RUDDER.—To dream of a broken Rudder portends indecision and distress. Do not take a voyage if you can avoid it for some time.

RUE.—Domestic difficulties.

RUINS.—It is a fortunate omen to dream that you are wandering amid the Ruins of some fine old building. If it is merely a modern house that has tumbled down, that is a bad sign. Beware of speculation.

RUMBLE.—To hear strange Rumbles from below the earth in a dream, such as those which precede an earthquake, is a sign of future trouble which it will take your utmost forethought to avert.

RUNNING.—This is generally an obstacle dream. If you succeed in reaching your goal, then all will go well. But if you tire, or stop Running, then expect business difficulties.

RUST.—Rust or neglect in your dreams is always a bad sign. Beware of loss through your own carelessness.

RUSTIC.—This is a fortunate dream, meaning that a busier life will soon be yours, one in which you can be truly successful.

RUSTLING.—To dream of hearing the Rustling of wings is one of the best omens and means that your future will be protected and happy.

RYE.—Eating Rye bread denotes popularity with the other sex.

S

SABLE.—The colour betokens tidings of loss; the fur is a warning against extravagance.

SACK.—An obstacle. If the Sack is full and you empty it, then all will go well. But an empty Sack shows some difficulty that will probably cause loss.

SACRIFICE.—A sign of coming festivities.

SADDLE.—To dream that you are riding a Horse without a Saddle, foretells ill-health through your own carelessness. Revise your plans at once and guard against mistakes.

SADNESS.—A good omen for your future; lasting joys.

SAILING.—This is another form of the Water dream, and the meaning depends upon whether the water is smooth and your voyage pleasant. If not, then expect trouble and worry, according to the severity of the storm in your dream. The smaller the Boat, the greater your success, or your misfortune.

SAILOR.—See **MARINER.**

SALAD.—Your own qualities will ensure your advancement in the world.

SALMON.—Family troubles.

SALT.—This is a fortunate dream in every way, but if you spill the Salt, you may expect some difficulty and hard work before you succeed.

SAND.—Many small vexations.

SAPPHIRE.—This is considered a fortunate dream, but it concerns your friends more than yourself.

SASH.—To dream of wearing one, a happy marriage.

SATIN or SILK.—A fortunate dream for the business man, but the lover should beware of false and flattering words.

SAUCEPAN.—See **POTS.**

SAUSAGE.—Domestic troubles, often through ill-health.

SAVAGE.—Small worries through the dishonesty of another. To dream of many Savages signifies rescue by a friend from a trouble of your own making.

SAVINGS.—To dream you are accumulating Savings foreshadows poverty.

SAW.—It is not a fortunate omen to dream that you are Sawing wood. At best, it indicates difficulties to be overcome.

SCALD or BURN.—A dream of contrary—good fortune will follow after the first difficulties have been overcome.

SCARLET.—See **COLOUR.**

SCENT.—See **PERFUME.**

SHOWERS.—A setback in your plans through a deceitful enemy.

SHROUD.—News of a wedding is at hand.

SIEVE.—Lost opportunities; make up your mind to grasp the next.

SIGH.—Cheerful company and a merry time.

SIGNATURE.—Loyal companions will uphold you at all times.

SIGNPOST.—Good advice will be given you; do not ignore it.

SIGNAL.—Waiting in a station for a train that is Signalled, is a portent of long delayed wishes that will at last be realised.

SILK.—See **SATIN.**

SILVER.—To dream of Silver is a sign of some loss. Do not be hasty in your plans. If the coins are of large value, you may escape if you are careful, but Sixpences and Threepenny-bits are a bad omen.

SINGING.—This is a dream of contrary, for it foretells of troubles to come, but they will soon pass, so do not despair. To dream that you hear other people Singing shows that the difficulties will come through your dealings with other people.

SINGLE.—For a married man or woman to dream of being Single again is a sign of jealousy and gossip which will cause you much worry. Be true and trustful and all will be well.

SIPHON.—A happy time in a pretty frock; many compliments. For a man this dream signifies an invitation to a bachelor party.

SINKING.—Bad news of a friend, and losses in business.

SISTERS.—To dream you see your Brothers and Sisters signifies long life.

SITTING.—Advancement in the world, especially if sitting on a high stool.

SITUATION.—See **OFFICE**.

SKIFF.—To watch one pass on a smooth river, a valued friend will rise out of your sphere. To see one in difficulties or upset, a business failure. To be in one rowing yourself, however, means achievements and gain.

SKATING.—Generally considered a warning of some coming danger.

SKELETON.—To dream that you see a Skeleton is a sign of domestic trouble. See **GHOST** and **BONES**.

SKIN.—Your own Skin, if healthy, good fortune; if it appears disfigured, kindness from those of whom you least expect it.

SKITTLES.—See **NINEPINS**.

SKULL.—An engagement is in the near future for you.

SCHOOL.—To dream you begin again to go to School, and cannot say your lessons right, shows you are about to undertake something you do not understand.

SCISSORS.—A warning of false friends. Beware of giving your confidence too fully.

SCRATCHED.—To dream of being Scratched foretells hurt.

SCREAM.—It is considered a fortunate sign to find yourself screaming in a dream.

SEA.—See **OCEAN, RIVER,** and similar words.

SEALS.—Uncertainty as to the result of a legal matter will vex you, but only for a short time.

SEAT.—To dream that one has fallen from his Seat, signifies that he shall be displaced from office.

SECRET.—To dream of a Secret being whispered in your ear means a public dignity to be bestowed on you.

SEE-SAW.—An unexpected love affair, which may not prove long-lasting.

SENTINEL.—New business introductions and a journey to the South.

SEPARATION.—To dream that you are Separated from those you love foretells the failure of some cherished plan.

SEPULCHRE.—Good news concerning a birth, and a letter will lead to great happiness.

SERPENT.—See **SNAKE.**

SERMON.—Approaching indisposition.

SERVANT.—For a woman to dream that she is a servant is an obstacle dream. Persevere and stick close to your job. To dream that you employ several Servants is an unfortunate omen.

SEW.—An obstacle dream. If your Sewing is successful, and you complete the garment or other article, all will be well. But if you leave off before finishing the work, then look out for troubles.

SHABBY.—New clothes will soon be yours when you dream of going about in Shabby ones.

SHADOW.—Money gained through legal affairs.

SHAMROCK.—News of long past matters will change your affairs.

SHARK.—This presages a narrow escape from serious trouble or illness.

SHAVE.—To dream that you are Shaving, or that some-else is Shaving you, is a warning of difficulty ahead. Be very careful whom you trust, and do not lend money, or buy shares and stocks.

SHAWL.—Deep affection from one you love.

SHEEP.—A fortunate dream, for it tells of coming success through well-conceived plans. See **LAMB.**

SHEIK.—Hard times are in store for you ; save while you can.

SHELF.—Your desires will be thwarted.

SHELL.—To dream of a Shell with the fish alive in it predicts prosperity, but an empty sea-shell is a bad omen.

SHEPHERD.—This is considered a bad omen, if you see no Sheep at the time. If the flock is there also, then the presence of the Shepherd increases your difficulties, but will not stop your ultimate success.

SHILLING.—A small disappointment of grievance.

SHINGLE.—Advancement in position.

SHIP.—To dream that you are travelling in a Ship shows good fortune if you reach your destination safely. See also **BOAT, OCEAN, SEA.**

SHIPWRECK.—A certain omen of disaster.

SHIRT or CHEMISE.—It is always a fortunate omen. when you dream of your Shirt or your Chemise. Good fortune follows your efforts.

SHIVER.—New garments will soon be yours, and they will be very much to your liking.

SHOES.—This might almost be called a dream of contrary, for if you see yourself without Shoes, then you may expect success in business. To dream that your Shoes are worn or patched is a certain sign of difficulties, but with care and hard work you will succeed. New Shoes show some fortunate enterprise, with unexpected results. See also **BOOTS.**

SHOOTING.—It is a very bad omen if you kill, or attempt to kill any living creature in your dream. To Shoot and miss shows some success over your difficulties.

SHOP.—To dream that you are keeping a Shop indicates hard work before you prosper; it depends to a great extent upon whether your dream Shop does good business.

SHORE.—Decide to see for yourself the person in your thoughts; you will not be disappointed.

SKY.—This is a fortunate dream unless you see heavy clouds. A few clouds merely show difficulties that you will probably overcome. But watch carefully whether the clouds are gathering or dispersing.

SLATE.—To write on one, new plans; to break one, your plans will fail.

SLAUGHTER.—You will attain a high position in the world.

SLEEP.—To dream you Sleep is evil.

SLEET.—Tedious company will demand your patience and an interesting disclosure will be made to you.

SLEEVE.—Much travel will be your lot in life.

SLEDGE.—Exciting times are in store for you, but do not be too venturesome.

SLIDING.—News of a wedding.

SLIPPERS.—A small kindness on your part will reap a large reward.

SMUGGLING.—This betokens a plan which will almost succeed but not quite.

SMALL-POX.—To dream of Small-pox denotes profit and wealth.

SMILING.—One of the very best of omens, whether you yourself are Smiling or whether you see someone else Smiling.

SMOKE.—Some present success, but you will not really benefit by it. The denser the Smoke, the greater will be your disappointment.

SNAKES.—This dream is a warning of treachery where you least expect it; some unfortunate turn of events that you have not anticipated. Your plans will be wrecked.

SNAILS.—Intemperance and inconstancy.

SNARES.—A change for the better.

SNEEZE.—Good fortune will attend your plans.

SNOW.—This is a very good dream, but you may have to work hard, especially if you find yourself walking in a Snowstorm. See also **HAIL**.

SNUFF.—Pleasant surroundings and a happy time ahead.

SOAP.—An unexpected encounter will result in a solution of the matters which have puzzled you.

SODA.—A sign of a contented life despite much labour.

SOLDIERS.—Loss of employment and probably many changes before you settle down once more.

SOLD.—To dream of being Sold is fair to those who are in poverty. But to the rich and the sick it is ill.

SOLES.—Misfortune and vexation.

SORROW.—See **LAMENT.**

SOP.—Be careful as to investments.

SOUP.—Speculations will turn out well.

SOUTH.—If you dream of a journey Southwards or of being in Southern places it is a good sign in love matters, but not in business.

SOWING SEEDS.—Avoid being involved in any uncertain matters such as speculations or lotteries.

SPADE.—A new vista of contentment will open before you. Keep to beaten tracks when out alone.

SPANGLES.—An invitation to a place of amusement.

SPARROWS.—These friendly little birds denote hard work, but with some success at the end.

SPARROW-HAWK.—Beware of your enemies. They are conspiring against you.

SPATS.—An influential man is attracted to you, but be on your guard.

SPEAR.—A good sign of worldly successes and renown to come soon.

SPECTACLES.—A short change of scene; beware of double-dealing from strangers.

SPELLING.—Success to all your plans.

SPENDING.—Be careful to economise for a time; money matters will improve after a long while.

SPIDER.—Good fortune is on the way, especially in your business ventures.

SPINNING.—Annoyance and anxiety; new acquaintances may prove untrustworthy.

SPONGE.—A portent of a highly placed admirer in the army or navy.

SPOTS.—An offer of promotion which you will do well to take.

SPRAY.—High walls and fine surrounding will come into your view in an interesting manner.

SPRING.—To dream of Spring in Winter is an omen of a wedding soon to take place.

SPY.—Adventure will come your way, but you have a protective influence near you and will meet with no harm.

SQUINT.—It is fortunate to dream of a man who squints; you have the affections of the one you love; but the reverse is true should the person in your dream be a woman.

SQUARES.—Chequered material or a pattern of Squares is a good sign of success.

SQUIRRELS.—Be content. Hard work is your lot, so keep cheerful and persevere.

STABLE.—A good companion will be yours for life.

STAG.—To see these noble animals is a good omen, but you must not molest or chase them, or you will ruin your own plans by your greed.

STAIN.—To dream of Stained garments presages scandal to their wearer.

STAIRS.—To descend a Staircase, your wish will be granted; to descend or tumble down them means the reverse.

STAMMER.—Fresh interests will lead to happiness.

STAMPS.—Association with someone in a high official position will cause you some worry but much gain.

STAR.—See **COMET.**

STARCHING.—To dream that you are Starching linen, shows you will be married to an industrious person.

STARVATION.—A dream of contrary, for it tells of success in business, or worldly affairs.

STATUES.—To dream of seeing Statues moving, signifies riches.

STEALING.—A gift of jewelley will be offered you.

STEAM.—Doubts and differences between you and one you love which only you can clear away.

STEEL.—A true and steadfast marriage partner unless the dream is of a knife, which means an enemy.

STEEPLE.—An unfortunate dream unless you think you are climbing one, which means achievement of your greatest wish.

STEPPING-STONES.—An omen of good fortune in love matters.

STEW.—A variety of presents will be made to you including one from a sweetheart.

STILE.—Walk warily, an enemy is trying to entrap you.

STILTS.—Pleasant views concerning children. Do not offend your associates by conceit or you may regret it.

STINGS.—Signify grief and care.

STOCKINGS.—To see them on: light colour, sorrow; dark, pleasure; a hole in one, you will lose something; woollen, affluence; silk, hardships.

STONES.—Angry discussions and new surroundings.

STOOP.—If you dream of Stooping to speak to someone it means a thrilling time followed by a quiet future.

STOOL.—To dream of sitting on a Stool means honour and achievement through your own merits.

STORKS.—A promise of ill-tidings.

STORM.—Another obstacle dream.

STOVE.—A burnt-out grate is a sign of hard times to come; but a Stove filled with burning coal foretells prosperity.

STRANGE PLACE.—A sign of inherited money soon to come to you.

STRANGERS.—A dream of contrary. If you dream of Strangers, the more of them the better, it means the assistance of kind friends, who will help you on in life.

STRANGLE.—To dream of being Strangled, trouble caused by the one you dream of; to think you are Strangling someone, your wish will come true.

STRAW.—A warning of difficulties. You must work hard in order to overcome your troubles.

STRAWBERRIES.—A sign of some unexpected success.

STREETS.—To dream of being in Streets which you have never seen before, many journeys and voyages, which will bring you prosperity.

STRING.—Strong powers of attraction are yours, which you must use carefully ; a voyage is in your near future.

STRUGGLE.—To dream of Struggling to escape from something or someone means great improvements in your health and strength.

STUMBLE.—This depends upon whether you actually fall. If so, expect trouble ; otherwise it is only an obstacle.

STUMPS.—To dream of knocking out cricket Stumps signifies a new friendship made within high walls and near water.

SUGAR.—This means sweet words and a happy future.

SUICIDE.—A sign of an overstrained mind and a warning to change your surroundings for a time.

SULK.—To dream of being Sulky forebodes poverty ; of a Sulky friend, a fickle sweetheart.

SUMMER.—" Dream of times out of season ; hear of things out of reason." If the dream comes in Winter, the above holds good, but it is not a sign of good fortune at any other time.

SUMMER-HOUSE.—Pleasant prospects for the future are indicated.

SUMMONS.—Adverse criticism and scandal will vex you.

SUMS.—If you cannot get them right, a dangerous friendship is portended, better broken.

SUN.—Success in money matters and in love. See also **COMET.**

SUNDAY.—A coming change of scene and interests.

SUNDIAL.—Coming events include a marriage and a death in your immediate circle.

SUNRISE.—This is a token of ambitions soon to be realised, while to dream of watching the sunset signifies the reverse.

SUPPER.—News of a birth.

SUNSTROKE.—To dream that you have this complaint means that you will be much envied and with reason.

SURF.—You will need all your tact to avoid the attentions of an unwelcome admirer.

SURGEON.—The slight illness of a friend will cause a deeper relationship between you.

SURPLICE.—Contentment to the married; marriage to the single.

SUSPENDERS.—Anxiety caused through your own careless words; a broken Suspender means an apology to be made.

SWALLOW.—Domestic happiness and faithful friends.

SWAN.—A good omen, but it only affects your business affairs.

SWARM.—A Swarm of bees means prosperity in the family.

SWEARING.—Bad language in a dream is always unfortunate, whether you are yourself to blame or someone else.

SWEEP.—To dream of a Sweep is an excellent omen; your plans can scarcely fail.

SWEEPING.—It is a sign of a happy domestic life if you find yourself Sweeping or cleaning a room in your dream.

SWEETHEART.—To dream that your lover is beautiful and pleasing to you, is a good omen; but be cautious if you dream that he or she is fickle and changeable.

SWEETS.—You will receive a bunch of flowers with a Sweet message hidden in them.

SWIMMING.—Hard work confronts you, but if you Swim to shore, or reach your objective, then you will succeed in the end.

SWING.—A change of plan will prove very successful in the long run. A gift of flowers will soon be made to you.

SWOON.—To dream you see a person Swoon, is unfortunate to the maid. To the married it is a sign they will become rich and prosperous.

SWORDS.—All sharp-edged weapons or tools indicate bad news.

T

TABLE.—It is not fortunate to be seated at a Table in your dream; but it is favourable if you see others thus seated.

TABLECLOTH.—It is a very good omen to see a clean white Tablecloth; but if it is dirty or soiled, then expect trouble of your own causing.

TABLEAU.—This is a sign of a frivolous wife or husband who will be fickle and too fond of amusement. Think well before you marry.

TACKS.—Your quick speech and sharp wit make you feared; be kind, unless you do not mind a lonely future.

TACKING-COTTON.—To dream of using quantities of Tacking-cotton presages new clothes for a joyful occasion.

TAFFETA.—Wealth that will bring no satisfaction.

TAILOR.—To a girl this dream signifies that she will marry an inferior.

TALISMAN.—To see a Talisman or charm warns the dreamer of danger on land. Walk carefully in crowded places.

TALK.—Family difficulties; serious if you hear loud voices.

TALONS.—If a creature with Talons should scratch you in a dream an enemy will triumph over you; but should it run away or fly, your enemies are powerless to hurt you.

TAMBOURINE.—Forebodes inconstancy in husband or sweetheart; be watchful or a rival will supplant you.

TANDEM.—To dream of driving horses in this manner signifies two lovers who will cause you difficulty through jealousy.

TAP.—To dream of a water Tap is a sign of a good income, especially if water is running freely from it.

TAPIOCA.—To cook it is a sign of luck in some small speculation; to eat in dreams is a warning of small losses.

TAPER.—If you dream of carrying a lighted Taper, it is the only burden you will ever carry, for wisdom and good fortune will protect your path.

TANGLE.—To dream of a Tangled skein of wool means difficult people to contend with; patience will, however, be well rewarded.

TAPESTRY.—Great enjoyment will come to you from small causes.

TAR.—To see a barrel of Tar merely presages travel; if on your clothes, much vexation through gossip.

TARGET.—Architectural plans will claim your attention. A change of residence.

TARTS.—To dream one makes Tarts signifies joy and delight.

TASSELS.—Cheerful company will visit you; many small gifts will please you.

TAXI.—Hasty news will be sent you; be on guard against false information.

TEA.—To dream that you are making or drinking Tea is a warning of many small difficulties ahead. Persevere and all will go well.

TEACHER.—If the dreamer is Teaching, an invitation to a solemn occasion is portended; if being taught, anger about a trifling slight will vex you.

TEAM.—To a townsman, success to your plans; to a farmer, a good harvest.

TEASE.—Your secret hopes will be discovered and much discussed, yet you will gain them in the end.

TEARS.—A sign of contrary—happiness awaits you.

TEETH.—It is always unfortunate to dream of your Teeth. Watch your health.

TELEGRAM.—It is more fortunate to receive a Telegram than to send one, but neither event is a happy omen.

TELESCOPE.—You are apt to exaggerate your troubles. Cares will lessen if they are faced cheerfully.

TEMPEST.—See **STORM.**

TEMPLE.—A foreign Temple is a portent of curious experiences to be yours before long. Discretion will bring you a big reward.

TEMPTATION.—Obstacles are barring your way to what should by rights be yours; guard your tongue and your good sense will surmount all difficulties.

TENT.—You will find great pleasure in helping the love-affairs of some youthful friends of yours.

TERRACE.—A rise in worldly position will befall you owing to a legacy.

TERRIER.—All dreams of Dogs signify friends, except when they snarl or bite, which forebodes quarrels.

THAW.—A former adversary will become your friend shortly.

THEATRE.—To dream that you witness a performance at the Theatre is a warning of treachery from someone whom you trust. Be cautious in discussing your plans, otherwise you will lose money.

THERMOMETER.—Life will be varied with many journeys and changes of position; better if the Thermometer register "Fair," and not so good if stormy weather be indicated.

THIEF or THIEVES.—This is a bad dream if you are robbed, and shows loss of money in any case. See **ROBBER.**

THIMBLE.—It is considered very fortunate for a woman to dream that she has lost her Thimble.

THINNESS.—If a girl dream that she has grown Thin, it predicts tears for a lost lover.

THREE.—To see Three birds flying, or ships sailing is a sign of a perilous journey to be taken, which you will, however, come safely through.

THRASH.—It is not a fortunate omen when you find yourself being Thrashed in a dream; but it is a good sign if you Thrash someone else.

THIRST.—Really an obstacle dream—if you satisfy your Thirst you will overcome your troubles.

THISTLES.—Quarrels which can be avoided if you are tactful.

THREAD.—To wind Thread denotes wealth gained by thrifty ways; to break it hard times; to unravel knotted Thread, a mystery solved.

THROAT.—It is generally considered a good sign if you dream of any trouble with your Throat.

THRONE.—You will lose valued friends in order to gain public distinctions.

THUMB.—This is a dream of obstacles in your path. If any injury to your Thumb prevents you from using your hand, then expect business losses.

THUNDER.—A Thunder Storm is a sign of great difficulties in store for you. Like all obstacle dreams, it depends upon what happens in your dream.

THYME.—Almost all herbs are a sign of good fortune, especially if they seem to be growing strongly or are in flower.

TIARA.—Should a girl dream of wearing a sparkling Diadem, it is a warning that her ambition is beyond her reach.

TICKET.—Good tidings long expected will come at last.

TICKLE.—A misunderstanding will be cleared up. If the Tickle be in the nose or throat, so that the dreamer sneeze, he will surely be asked to lend money.

TIDE.—To dream of seeing a strong Tide flowing in, is a sign of favourable circumstances soon to happen

TIGER.—Another obstacle dream—if you are caught by the wild beast, look out for heavy losses. See **LION** and **LEOPARD.**

TILES.—Be careful of accidents with tools, especially should the Tile fall and break.

TILL.—To dream of a shop Till filled with coins betokens a wealthy trader for a husband or a well-dowered woman for a wife; an empty Till is a warning of dishonest servants.

TIMBER.—To fell Timber is a presage of a long engage-

ment ending in a happy marriage, unless the Timber seem to be old and rotten, in which case the engagement will be broken.

TIN.—A dream signifying that counterfeit friendship will be taken for true. Test your friends before you trust them.

TINKER.—Do not meddle in a friend's affairs after you have dreamed of a Tinker, or you will do more harm than good.

TIPTOE.—A slight tiff will part you from one you love if you do not take care to make up a quarrel before nightfall.

TIRED.—Take no risks with your business affairs. You are in danger of losses.

TOADS or FROGS.—Loss and difficulties are shown, but if the creature hops away, hard work may save the situation.

TOAST.—This is a favourable sign presaging true friends and homely joys in the family circle.

TOBACCO.—Your fancied troubles will soon vanish like smoke.

TOBOGGAN.—You will soon be involved in someone else's affairs so deeply that it will be difficult to extricate yourself. Be careful of every step.

TOMATOES.—A portent of comfortable circumstances which you will attain by your own efforts.

TOMBS.—To dream that you are walking among Tombs foretells marriages ; to dream that you are ordering your own Tomb denotes that you will shortly be married ; but to see that Tomb fall into ruins denotes sickness and trouble to your family. To dream that you, with another person, are admiring Tombs, denotes your future partner to be very suitable for you. To dream you are inspecting the Tombs of the illustrious dead denotes your speedy advancement to honour and wealth.

TONGS.—This is a dream of warning against both fires and quarrels.

TONGUE.—Unlike the Throat, it is an unfavourable omen if you dream of any trouble with your Tongue.

TOOTHACHE.—You will have much to be grateful for in a letter from a distant friend.

TORCH.—This signifies that if you will hold the light of reason to your troubles you will quickly see your way out of them.

TORNADO.—A dream warning you against strife in your home or in business. It will surely bring disaster in either.

TORPEDO.—A presage of love at first sight, which will completely alter your life.

TORRENT.—Do not rush at things too violently; power is not the only good thing in the world. If you cross the Torrent in your dream, you will accomplish your aims.

TORTOISE or TURTLE.—Long life and success.

TORTURE.—To dream of being Tortured signifies domestic bliss.

TOURNAMENT.—Excellent news and a healed quarrel are denoted.

TOWEL.—You will undergo a brief illness, but will recover very quickly.

TOWN.—For a country dweller to dream of a large Town is a warning against dangerous ambitions, but for a townsman, increased business and gain is signified.

TOWER.—The higher you ascend, the greater your loss will be. It is an obstacle dream.

TOYS.—This dream indicates that your family will be very clever and successful.

TRAFFIC.—Many friends and some public dignity are promised.

TRAMP.—An absent friend is thinking of you. A letter from that friend is on its way.

TRAP-DOOR.—A surprising and unpleasant letter, together with the loss of an important key, will worry you. Look for the latter in a wooden hiding-place.

TRAIN.—See **TRAVEL.**

TRAVEL.—Difficulties in your business ventures. Success depends upon hard work.

TREACLE.—You will hear pleasant words, which will certainly stick in your memory.

TREAT.—Financial affairs will prosper for you, owing to the good influence of one much above you.

TREASURE.—It is a most unfortunate omen to dream that you have discovered Treasure. Beware of treachery among those you trust.

TREES.—If you dream of Trees in full leaf, it is a very fortunate omen, for nature is kind to you. If you see a Tree cut down, then expect loss in business. To dream of climbing Trees is a certain omen of hard work and little luck, whatever happens in your dream.

TRELLIS.—A firm friendship will prove the foundation of your success in life.

TRENCH.—An evil influence is near you; do not be entrapped.

TRESPASS.—To dream you are on forbidden premises presages a very strong attraction towards one who is already married. There is the utmost danger in this friendship and your dream is the warning sent you.

TRIAL.—You have an admirer whose merits you have not hitherto valued. You would be wise to study and develop this friendship.

TRIANGLE.—You will have to choose between two lovers.

TRIDENT.—The girl who dreams of a Trident will most certainly be loved by a sailor.

TRIGGER.—You will receive compliments upon your abilities and these may shortly lead to advancement.

TRINKETS.—Your loved one is vain and fickle. Do not wear your heart upon your sleeve.

TRIPE.—A rival in business is trying to steal your position. Be watchful and attentive to your own interests.

TRIPLETS.—You are very unlikely to have such an occurrence in your life or family if you dream of them.

Instead, you will have cause to regret your lack of home ties.

TRUNCHEON.—To dream of wielding this is a warning against thieves.

TRUNK.—A traveller will return from abroad. A wish will be granted in connection with a home.

TRYST.—A reconciliation or a re-established friendship will end romantically.

TRUMPET or CORNET.—It is considered fortunate to hear the call of Trumpets in your dream.

TROUT.—Your troubles will vanish.

TROUBLE.—If you find yourself in Trouble in your dream, it is a sign of change of residence.

TROUSERS.—This dream signifies flirtations to the married, and quarrels to the single dreamer.

TUB.—Hard times, if empty, but better days to come if full.

TUG.—Merry company and a wedding between middle aged lovers.

TULIP.—A short engagement and a secret marriage will be the fate of the girl who dreams of Tulips.

TUMBLER.—To drink from a clean Tumbler denotes health and activity ; from a dirty one, the reverse.

TUNNEL.—Another obstacle dream. If you do escape from the Tunnel all will go well.

TURKEY.—Trouble with your friends and with your business customers or associates.

TURNIPS.—Disappointment and vexation.

TURTLE.—These curious creatures are an omen of an unfulfilled wish or ambition. Hard work may succeed.

TWINE.—A tiff with a friend over a very small matter will cause you tears. Avoid flirting and jealousy.

TWINS.—Babies are not considered fortunate omens in a dream, though young children are favourable. Twin babies make the omen more dangerous.

U

UGLINESS.—It is a fortunate omen to dream of an Ugly person.

UMBRELLA.—See **PARASOL.**

UNCLE.—See **AUNT.**

UNDERTAKER.—This is one of the "contrary" dreams, and denotes a wedding.

UNDRESS.—If you dream of being in public not fully dressed, be cautious of word and act, or gossip will distress you.

UNFAITHFUL.—A dream of contrary. All will go well with your future, if you dream that your lover, husband, or wife is Unfaithful.

UNHAPPY.—A dream of contrary. The more miserable you are in your dream, the better for you in real life.

UNFORTUNATE (Being So).—Care will bring success.

UNICORN.—To dream of fabulous creatures presages anxiety caused by falsehoods.

UNIFORM.—This dream signifies a chance of promotion which will bring you the utmost good fortune in love as well as a better position.

UNION JACK.—This is an excellent dream denoting a chance to go abroad with a faithful marriage partner.

UNIVERSITY.—A sign that you are fortunate in your talents and in your friends.

UNKIND.—To dream of the Unkindness of one you love means the reverse. Your affection is as deeply returned.

UNLOCK.—A discovery will be made in your home ; do not try to keep a secret from those who love you.

UNMARRIED.—For married people to dream of being single again is a sign of danger from jealousy and gossip. Be true, and trust each other and all will be well.

UPROAR.—To dream of scenes of confusion and Uproar signifies a decision which will be arrived at soon after long delay; it will be as you wish.

URN.—This portends news of very young relations who will achieve great distinction much to your pride and delight.

V

VACCINATION.—You are in danger of giving more affection than its recipient is worth; keep a guard on your heart and obey your head.

VALENTINE.—This predicts news of an old sweetheart who still thinks much of you.

VALLEY.—To dream that you are in a Valley is a warning of ill-health. Do not overtax your powers.

VAMPIRE.—A bad omen; you will marry for money and find it a bad bargain.

VANS.—Do not act on the impulse of the moment; all things come to one who waits.

VASE.—You are apt to give too much thought to appearances; try to value useful qualities in one who loves you.

VAT.—To dream of a full Vat indicates that you will always have a fund of wisdom and wealth at your disposal; an empty Vat signifies your need for both in the near future.

VAULT.—To dream that you are in a Vault is a sign of difficulties in your path. If eventually you escape, all will be well once more. But be careful of undertaking new ventures.

VEAL.—Certain good fortune.

VEGETABLES.—Hard work for little result will surely follow a dream of these Green offerings of Nature. Persevere and do not lose heart.

VEIL.—To dream that you are wearing a Veil is a bad omen, even if it is a Bridal Veil, unless you remove it before the dream is concluded.

VELVET.—A fortunate dream, but it will depend largely upon the colour. See **COLOUR.**

VENISON.—To dream about Venison, denotes change in affairs. To dream you eat it signifies misfortune.

VERDICT.—Hasty preparations for a land journey caused by the good fortune of a friend.

VERMIN.—Nearly all unpleasant dreams of this sort go by " contraries " and mean good luck.

VERSES.—This means that you will not succeed if you work alone ; take a partner.

VEST.—There is hostility around you ; guard your actions and conceal your suspicions if you would overcome it.

VEXATION.—Foretells prosperity.

VICAR.—As with all Church officials, this is not a fortunate omen.

VICTORIA CROSS.—To dream you are presented with this honour is a sign that you will win your good fortune by merit alone.

VICTORY.—This is an omen of failure through strife ; do not take sides in other people's quarrels.

VICTUALS.—To help others to food denotes social pleasures ; to eat in dreams signifies loss of business.

VIEW.—To dream of a beautiful and sunlit scene presages a most fortunate future.

VIGIL.—To dream of keeping a long Vigil is a sign of hope deferred, but sure to be fulfilled in the end.

VILLA.—To dream that you are going over a fine Villa is a sign that you will be very happy in a small one before long.

VILLAGE.—This dream promises an offer of a change which will prove most important to your future.

VILLAIN.—To dream of a Ruffian or Villain denotes a letter or present from one you love.

VINEGAR.—Useless toil.

VINTAGE.—Successful business operations and affection rewarded.

VINE.—One of the most fortunate dreams, especially if the Vine is in full leaf. You may have to work hard, but success is certain to come.

VIOLETS.—Very fortunate for the lover.

VIOLENCE.—If you are Violently attacked it portends better times for you ; to see Violence to others means festivities amongst cheerful friends.

VIOLIN.—To hear sweet music is a sign of social and domestic happiness, but beware if one of the strings should break, for it foretells a quarrel.

VIRGIN.—To dream of an effigy of the Virgin is a warning of threatened trouble ; be reserved and on guard with all but trusted friends.

VISION.—Danger to the person who appears to you.

VISIT.—To pay a Visit, obstacles to your plans ; to receive a Visit from a friend signifies travel for pleasure.

VISITORS.—It is not a good omen to dream of Visitors ; the more people there are around you, the greater will be your business difficulties. See **STRANGERS.**

VOICE.—To hear people speaking is a dream of contrary. If they appear to be happy and merry, then expect reverses in business and many worries.

VOLCANO.—To dream of a Volcano foretells great disagreements, family jars, and lovers' quarrels. To a man of commerce it portends dishonest servants, and a robbery or some sad convulsion. To lovers it is a sign that all deceit, intrigue, base designs, on one side or the other will be exploded, and the designer will be branded with the contempt and execration so justly deserved.

VOLLEY.—This signifies opposition from several sources. You will have to make every effort to overcome it.

VOLUNTEER.—If you dream you are a Volunteer, you will be a soldier and lose your life in battle.

VOMIT.—To dream of Vomiting, whether of blood,

meat or phlegm, signifies to the poor, profit ; to the rich, hurt.

VOTING.—You must be more confident if you wish to fulfil your hopes ; you are favoured but too diffident.

VOW.—To dream of a broken vow is bad to all.

VOYAGE.—A message from a distance is soon to be received.

VULTURE.—Dangerous enemies : (To kill)—conquest of misfortune ; (To see one devouring its prey)—your troubles will cease and fortune smile upon you.

W

WADDING.—To see or use quantities of Wadding in a dream is a sign that health troubles will cause you to become very thin. Your business, however, will prosper.

WADDLE.—To see birds that usually swim, Waddling on land signifies that uncertain matters will be satisfactorily concluded.

WADE.—It is considered a good sign for lovers if they dream of Wading in clear water. If the water is muddy or rough, disillusion will soon come.

WAFER.—Should you dream of sealing a letter with a Wafer, legal matters will benefit you.

WAFTED.—To dream of moving in the air without wings is a sign of small vexations.

WAGER.—This portends losses. Act cautiously.

WAGON.—To dream that you are driving in a Wagon is a sign of loss of money. But if a loaded Wagon or cart comes to your door, then some unexpected good fortune will come.

WAGES.—To receive them, danger of small thefts ; to pay them, money from a legacy.

WAILING.—To dream you hear Wailing and weeping

from unseen voices is a bad sign of loss of someone dear to you.

WAINSCOT.—To dream that you hear a mouse in the Wainscotting of a house portends a good friend in humble circumstances.

WAIST.—To dream of putting a belt around your Waist is an omen of unexpected money; to fasten anything round the Waist of another, you will be able to assist that person before long.

WAITS.—To dream of hearing the Waits at Christmas time is a sign of a happy romance, especially if there is snow on the ground in your dream.

WAITER.—To dream of being at a table where you are Waited upon is a sign of an invalid whom you will have to nurse shortly.

WALLET.—This portends important news from an unexpected source.

WALLFLOWERS.—To see and smell these flowers is a sign that you will be sought after, especially if you see them growing in a wall.

WALKING.—Small worries that will vanish if you tackle them bravely.

WALKING-STICK.—You will be given assistance in a great difficulty.

WALLS.—These are obstacles, and if you climb over them, all will be well with you. But you will have to face hard work.

WALNUTS.—All Nuts show small difficulties that need not prove serious if attacked earnestly. See **FRUIT.**

WALTZ.—An admirer is concealing his affection from you. Be kind.

WANDERING.—A good sign of advancement in your dearest hopes.

WAR.—To dream of War and affairs of War, signifies trouble and danger.

WARBLE.—To hear birds Warbling is a sign of happiness in love.

WARDER.—To dream of a prison Warder is a

" contrary " dream, signifying a happy holiday soon to come.

WAREHOUSE.—A dream of good omen. You will be successful in business and married life.

WARTS.—To see Warts on your hands in a dream indicates as many sums of money as you can see Warts, will come to you ; on the hands of others, signifies rich friends.

WASHING.—A dream of difficulties ahead, probably connected with friends or with your home life.

WASPS or BEES.—Enemies among those whom you trust.

WATER.—See **RIVER, OCEAN, SEA.**

WATCH.—A journey by land.

WATER-CARRIER.—Money increases.

WATER-CRESS.—Danger in love affairs, especially if you pick them from the water.

WATERFALL.—An invitation to a place of amusement. You are observed and gossiped about.

WATCHING.—To dream of Watching from a window or high places signifies you are being spied upon. If you have secrets, guard them well.

WATER-LILIES.—Your wish is out of reach ; do not try to gain it, lest further loss ensue.

WATCHMAN.—You are protected by silent love and friendship near you.

WATERMILL.—To dream of being in a Watermill is a favourable omen. To the tradesman it denotes great increase of business ; to the farmer, abundant crops ; in love, success, a rich sweetheart and happy marriage.

WATER-WHEEL.—To see a Water-wheel working, additional work will bring you new friends and more money.

WAVES.—See **WATER.**

WAYFARER.—To dream of meeting a Wayfarer on a lonely path is a sign of a new friend.

WAX.—Neither borrow nor lend money. You will have occasion to do both shortly. Try to avoid it.

WEASEL.—Beware of those who would appear to befriend you without reason.

WEATHERCOCK.—Uncertainty, changes and vexations.

WEATHER-VANE.—An excellent omen for trade, but not for love affairs.

WEAVING.—A wedding-dress will soon be made for you. Good news will be received in a letter.

WEB.—Travel and gratified wishes. A sign of wealth.

WEDDING.—A dream of contrary—expect trouble in your family circle.

WEDDING-RING.—A parting. To take it off in a dream means the parting will be final.

WEIGHTS.—Fresh work in new scenes, much discussion and planning.

WEEDS.—See **NETTLE.**

WEEDING.—Happiness and good fortune.

WEEPING.—To dream one weeps is joy and mirth.

WELL.—(To draw water) success and profit. (To fall in) danger that can scarcely be avoided.

WEST.—To dream of places in the far West, or on the side, sign of a coming journey.

WHALE.—Misunderstandings which will be cleared up in time. A delayed wedding is indicated.

WHEAT.—See **CORN.**

WHEELS.—Property will be left to you.

WHEAT-FIELD.—A sign of prosperous trade and a happy family.

WHIP.—An affectionate message. Good tidings will come shortly.

WHIRLPOOL.—Advice will be given to you well-worth following. An inheritance in the future.

WHIRLWIND.—Beware of dangerous reports.

WHISPERING.—A rumour will be confirmed. Financial gains are at hand.

WHIST.—To dream of playing the game means a better position.

WHISTLE.—To hear, scandal is being spread about you ;

to dream that you are Whistling merrily indicates sad news coming.

WHISKY.—This is a foreboding of ill; it signifies debts and difficulties.

WHITEWASH.—Introductions in gay company.

WHITE.—See **COLOUR.**

WIG.—Two proposals soon to come. The darker man loves you best.

WIDOW.—To dream that you are conversing with a Widow foreshadows that you will lose your wife by death. For a woman to dream that she is a Widow portends the infidelity of her husband. For a young woman to dream that she has been married, and becomes a Widow, prognosticates that her lover will abandon her.

WIDOWER.—To dream that you are one, denotes the sickness of your wife. For a young woman to dream that she is married to a Widower denotes much trouble with false lovers; but she will be happily married at last to a man of good sense and good conduct.

WIFE.—See **HUSBAND.**

WILDERNESS.—A festive occasion in your home. Keep to old friends.

WILLOW.—Do not trust a new acquaintance. Good news of someone dear to you.

WILL.—Dreaming of making your Will signifies that you will live a long time in happiness and joy.

WINCH.—A disappointment; unexpected good news to follow.

WIND.—Good news is coming; the stronger the gale of Wind, the sooner you may expect good fortune.

WINDMILL.—Some gain, but only of a small character.

WINE.—A sign of comfortable home life; it does not refer to business or love affairs.

WINGS.—A bad dream; you will lose money.

WINTER.—To dream of a Wintry scene with snow on the ground is an omen of prosperity, but to dream of Summer in Winter is the reverse.

WIRELESS.—Unexpected good news about money.

WISHING WELL.—Two admirers are seeking your company. Choose carefully.

WITNESS.—To dream of being a Witness in court is a warning to be on your guard against false accusations which will be made against you.

WITCH.—An ill-omen in every way.

WIZARD.—Family prosperity and contentment.

WOLF.—Enmity. (To kill) success ; (To pursue) dangers overcome ; (Pursued by) danger.

WOMAN.—To see many Women in a dream, wealth and renown ; a beautiful Woman, a happy marriage ; an ugly Woman, worry and vexation ; a Woman's voice, changes in position.

WOOD.—See **FOREST.**

WOODCUTTER.—Your efforts will not result in much profit.

WOOL.—Always a very fortunate omen. Success will be yours, both at home and in business.

WORKHOUSE.—A big legacy to come soon.

WORKMAN.—Your enterprise will bring great profit.

WORKSHOP.—A sign of good fortune.

WORMS.—Danger of infectious diseases.

WORSTED.—To wind it, a comfortable income ; to knit with it, you will inherit more than you earn.

WOUNDS.—To dream that you are Wounded is a favourable omen.

WREATH.—See **FLOWERS.**

WRECK.—Threatened trouble to health or business.

WREN.—To dream of this little bird is good.

WRESTLING.—An unfortunate dream, for it means loss of money through ill-health.

WRINKLES.—Compliments and social pleasures.

WRIST.—To dream that your Wrists are broken is very good ; it foretells that you will marry your present lover and be happy.

WRITING.—Written or printed matter is always unfavourable. If you dream that you are writing, you are creating difficulties by your own actions.

Y

YACHT.—To see one means good luck if the sea be smooth ; to be in one, ambitions realised, unless the sea be rough, which means disappointment.

YANKEE.—A renewed friendship with one from whom you have long been parted.

YARD.—News of an engagement amongst your friends. The wedding will bring you a new admirer.

YARN.—You will receive a fine present from an un-expected quarter.

YAWNING.—An obstacle dream, but not of serious import.

YEARNING.—To dream of a strong feeling of longing means that you will be indifferent where you would like to be kind.

YEAST.—Money which has been accumulated by thrift will be left to you under strange conditions.

YELL.—To dream of hideous Yells and noises is a sign of peace after strife. An introduction will alter your plans.

YIELD.—To dream of Yielding to persuasive words is a warning against pride ; do not believe flatterers.

YEW-TREE.—This dream denotes the death of an aged person, or relation, or patron, from whom you will receive a legacy which will place you above want. If you dream that you sit under a Yew-tree, it foretells that your life will not be long. But if you merely gaze upon it and admire it, it is a sign that you will live long.

YOKE.—You are too much under the influence of an older person. Try to develop your own personality.

YOLK.—To beat Egg-yolks in a dream is a good sign of money gained in a speculation or lottery.

YOUNG.—To dream that you have become Young

again is a favourable omen. But the change for the better will not last long.

YULE-TIDE.—A hasty wooing from a new admirer will end happily ; business and health matters will improve around you.

Z

ZEBRA.—Disagreement with friends.

ZEPPELIN.—A dream signifying an ambition far beyond your reach.

ZIG-ZAG.—This means many changes of mind and mood ; do not hesitate too long.

ZINC.—Your future will be built on firm foundations and your romance will be a long lasting one.

ZOOLOGICAL GARDENS.—Although wild animals in captivity are not generally good signs in themselves, it is considered fortunate to visit a Zoological Gardens.

ZULU.—To see Zulu natives surrounding you in a dream is a sign of release from a danger that has threatened your health and happiness.

Opening
doors to
the World
of books

Book
Tokens

Book Tokens
can be
bought and
exchanged
at most
bookshops